The Simple Epicure

Miranda Weston-Smith has cooked with passion since the age of fifteen. She has served her time as a kitchen slave in a Cornish restaurant and sold her own produce in a farm shop. Today, she divides her time between writing about science and cooking, thereby demonstrating that excellent food need not be the exclusive work of full-time professionals. She lives in Cambridge with her husband and young son.

Clare Newbolt trained at the Camberwell School of Art and Crafts and has lived and worked as an artist in Italy and the USA, where her work has been exhibited. She now lives in Swaffham Prior and continues to exhibit and work to commission as an illustrator.

The Simple Epicure

Stylish Food Without Fuss

MIRANDA WESTON-SMITH

Drawings by Clare Newbolt

ROBERT HALE · LONDON

Robert Hale Limited
Clerkenwell House
Clerkenwell Green
London EC1R 0HT

British Library Cataloguing in Publication Data

Weston-Smith, Miranda
   The simple epicure: stylish food without
   fuss.
   1. Cookery, International
   I. Title
   641.5   TX725.A1

   ISBN 0-7090-3000-2

Book design by Wendy Bann

Set in Goudy Old Style by
Rowland Phototypesetting Limited
Bury St Edmunds, Suffolk
Printed in Great Britain by
St Edmundsbury Press Limited
Bury St Edmunds, Suffolk
and bound by Woolnough Bookbinders Limited

Contents

For my brother
Hugh
who asked me to write it

Introduction

The purpose of this book is to give pleasure to you and your friends. I have tried to explain how to produce excellent food with the minimum of fuss and bother.

There are two principal ways of expanding your gastronomic experiences and pleasure. Either you can dress up familiar ingredients in novel ways and put your energy into executing elaborate methods for preparing and cooking food, or you can experiment with new materials, trying unusual combinations of raw ingredients such as grilling mackerel and serving it with leeks and watercress, or roasting a joint of pork and then setting it on cabbage spiced with chillis. This is the style of cooking I have developed in this book. Its purpose is to provide distinctive and memorable food that is quickly and easily prepared.

The key to success in this system lies, I believe, in simplicity: careful mixing of a very few ingredients can produce dramatic effects, but if there are too many, confusion and competition occur. It's rather like mixing oil paints on an artist's palette, and the dangers are the same: a few colours, thoughtfully combined, can create something new and striking but many will produce not a glorious hue but dull brown. Our palates can be confused in exactly the same way by a plethora of tastes and smells. The way to avoid this is to focus on just a few flavours in a dish, considering how they will complement and enhance one another.

Now set before your eyes the imaginary dishes of a meal and sample each one in turn. Do they too complement each other? Just like the figures in an oil painting, it is important that the individual dishes of a meal set each other off to their best advantage, avoiding glaring mismatches of colour or flavour, or repetition. You have probably eaten the kind of meal that Frances Partridge describes in her wartime diary (*A Pacifist's War*, 1978): 'An enormous all-beige meal, starting with beige soup thickened to the consistency of paste, followed by beige mince full of lumps and garnished with beige beans and a few beige potatoes, thin beige apple stew and a sort of skilly.' The modern version would run something like this: onion soup, an over-cooked chicken casserole with limp vegetables followed by a mousse of undefinable taste with airy cream. All the dishes are soft and fairly liquid and probably rather insipidly coloured. How much better it would be to have introduced contrasting flavours, richness, colour and texture into the menu.

I have sketched out some menus on p. 13, but here are some general guidelines.

First, if a meal were to begin with a soup, it would be best to follow it with a dish in which the ingredients are clearly discernible, such as a roast, rather than a stew in which the ingredients tend to break up; this might be followed by fruit or a tart.

Vegetables, salads and fruits give dishes colour but many sauces and purées lack the brilliance of their constitutents. A lot of meat can come out of the oven a slightly unappetizing brownish colour. Fish does not do much better. So that is why a wedge of lemon and a suggestion of parsley or watercress make a trout more appealing: you are stimulated by its appearance as well as its presumed flavour.

Rich food is most enjoyable when it is set in a puritan framework. Again it's a question of contrast: how can you appreciate a luscious chocolate pudding if you have already feasted on avocados and roast duck? The pudding would just be a burden at the end of such a meal. On the other hand it would be a joy after grilled fish or a salad. These remarks stem purely from aesthetics; they do not derive from any fads about fats and diet, although I think it is fairly generally agreed that it is a good idea to keep one's fat-consumption down.

For good measure I have thrown in a little of the science behind culinary operations. I hope this will be useful, particularly when things go wrong, as they do for everybody at some time. But mistakes can be turned to advantage: they give you insights into cooking, and so it is very important to learn from yours and other people's, to analyse what went wrong and set it right next time. For this reason, and others, you might find it helpful to keep a record in a notebook of your culinary explorations: the triumphs and the ones you want to forget. And remember that recipes aren't always perfect – maybe some of mine could be improved.

Acknowledgements

First, to my husband, Horace Barlow, I give very special thanks; this book owes much to him, and he has eagerly shared my culinary adventures. Second, my self-adopted culinary godmother is Daphne Henrion, and it was she who gave me enthusiasm for cooking – and many delicious meals – while I was a teenager. I would also like to give warm thanks to Clare Newbolt, who has illustrated this book so thoughtfully, and to Eric Glass.

Notes on the recipes

In case you aren't familiar with the customary culinary abbreviations for spoon measures, here they are:

tsp = teaspoon (the average capacity of a household teaspoon is 3 ml but the British Standard Measure, which is used by chemists, is 5 ml)
dsp = dessertspoon
tbs = tablespoon
and
3 tsp = 1 dsp
5 tsp = 1 tbs
8 tbs = ¼ pt/140 ml

Unless I have indicated to the contrary, all spoon measures should be level.

I have also used liquid volume and weight measurements, and both of these are given in the imperial and metric scales.

People vary a great deal in the quantity of salt they add to food, and so my figures are only intended to be recommendations.

Oven settings are stated in gas numbers (regulo) and fahrenheit and centigrade temperatures.

Most of the recipes yield six helpings, and the number is given at the beginning of each set of instructions. One helping is meant to represent the average quantity one person will consume, but while some may tuck away two or even three helpings, others nibble; for example, a lumberjack has at least twice the appetite of a sedentary student or office-bound executive. So it is wise to consider how many actual helpings you need to prepare when cooking for others who may have requirements different from yours.

Sometimes the quantities may be dictated by the nature of the raw ingredients or style of the dish. For example, smallish chickens are, to my mind, the best, and they yield about five helpings. If you wish to feed more people, I would recommend you buy two birds rather than one large one. Similarly many people don't have pots large enough to make six adequate helpings of mixed fried rice, and the fresh character will be lost the longer it is cooked; so the recipe is for four. By all means try altering the quantities for a recipe, but consider the consequences first.

I have attempted to order the recipes according to how difficult they are to execute. Those that are easiest I have placed first and then followed on with the more tricky ones. On the principle that simplicity should take precedence, those that require the use of electrical equipment are placed last.

You will find the operations much easier if you read the recipes through the day before you put them into action, to check you have the right ingredients and familiarize yourself with the method. Simple practicalities may determine this if your days are such that you can't fit in purchasing and cooking and entertaining all on one day. For each recipe I have given a preparation and cooking time, and this should help you plan your labours. In addition I have indicated when a recipe, or part of it, may be prepared in advance. (You will probably find that the preparation times become shorter as you become more adept and that is why I have given them a five minute leeway.) Of course, it will also vary with the circumstances: if you are sharing a kitchen with others or the 'phone keeps on ringing at critical moments, you will be slowed down.

One of the sources of variation in cooking times is the number of pots in an oven at any one time. Every item that is cooler than the oven is a heat-drain, and because few ovens have perfect thermostats, it means that the times will be marginally longer the more you have in an oven – you will learn to gauge this with experience. Timings will also be affected by quantities. If you have doubled a recipe, it will take longer to cook because of the extra bulk; it probably won't take double the time, more like half as long again if it is a stew or baked dish. Halving a recipe has a similar effect, and again it's not strictly proportional because there is the dish itself to heat up. So allow about three-quarters of the cooking time if you halve the quantities.

If you rarely cook for other people, your stores may be rather sparse – and strange. Here are some hints for provisions you could try keeping regularly so you are well armed with basic ingredients:

salt

black pepper (preferably as corns to be ground)

olive oil (extra virgin is the best)

peanut or other vegetable oil

plain flour

self-raising flour

caster sugar (don't bother with granulated because caster can be used for everything while the coarser granulated is unsuitable for many things)

rice

pasta

dried beans

split lentils

French mustard

stoned olives

tin of anchovies

tomato paste

almond flakes

raisins/currants

cooking wine

cheap brandy

potatoes (keep them dry and in the dark)

onions

garlic

fresh ginger root
fresh green chillis
dried herbs: dill weed
        basil
        mint leaves
        mixed
milk

cream
butter
bread
cheese: Cheddar
       Parmesan
       Gruyère or Emmenthal

Notes on some foods and cooking terms are on p. 133.

A final word on equipment. It is well worth investing in a really sharp knife (one that cuts food, not you), a wooden chopping-board, a garlic-crusher, a pepper-grinder, a heavy stewing-pot, a baking-dish and some non-stick saucepans. I say non-stick rather than the older kind because, though they are a little more expensive, they are so much easier to use and clean, and you can cook anything in them: you won't be forever looking for the one saucepan you can make sauces etc in. I hope you have a weighing machine and a liquid measurer as well as a colander. Most of the recipes require no electrical equipment; I think you will agree that it's perfectly possible to produce good food without modern gadgets.

Menus

One of the problems of cooking for other people is keeping them happy, and yourself. For this reason it's generally best not to have too many things that have to be done at the last moment, and if possible much of the preparation should be done in advance; it is quite taxing to produce one, or even two, hot dishes single-handed. Here are some suggestions:

Winter Menus

Prawn and rice salad
Roast pork with cabbage
Pears in red wine jelly

Chicken liver pâté
Haddock with mint sauce
Fresh fruit salad

Spicy snacks
Cauliflower Italian style
Almond meringues with cream

Goats' cheese toasts
Baked trout
Banana islands in plum sauce

Kipper pâté
Roast leg of lamb with green peppercorns
Baked apples

Salad Miranda
Roast beef with Yorkshire pudding
Appassionata

Grilled mackerel with leeks and watercress
Bakewell tart

Summer Menus

Chilled tomato and coriander soup
Baked salmon trout
Mollon's peaches

Salad of pasta
Chicken livers with dill
Gooseberry sorbet

Smoked salmon Thai style
Chicken breasts with lemon
Blackcurrant meringue

Globe artichokes with melted butter
Boiled gammon with parsley sauce
Fresh fruit salad

Oriental broth
Grilled halibut
Chocolate and ratafia pudding

Tagliatelle with mushrooms
Cucumber and avocado salad
Walnut ice-cream with ginger sauce

Prawn and cabbage ragoût
Cardamom cake with cream

Advice on wine

Nowadays a good selection of wines is usually available from local wine shops and supermarkets, but if you are in a remote spot it is well worth joining one of the wine clubs or societies that specialize in selling, and delivering by mail order. Making your choice of what to buy is difficult (and perhaps the more difficult the more you enjoy it), but remember the following points:

1) There is a rock-bottom price for a bottle of wine set by taxes, transportation charges etc. In the range from this to, say, double the price, the quality improves rapidly, and you usually get value for money.

2) Wine from countries (such as Spain, Portugal, Australia, New Zealand and those of Eastern Europe and South America) that are trying to build up their exports of table wine often offer products that are very good value. On the other hand it takes a lot to beat the cheaper wines from the real professionals in France (especially Bordeaux), Germany and California (the main source of modern wine-making techniques).

3) You will find that wine for drinking with food requires a bit of body and taste; bouquet, smoothness and mellowness are less important, and above all it should not be insipid.

4) If you have a local supplier, ask his advice, and tell him later if you agree with it – he should appreciate such feedback. Alternatively read the columns in magazines and Sunday newspapers.

5) Trust your own judgement and repeat your successes. Then try something new when the time comes for a change, knowing you can always fall back on an old favourite.

More specific suggestions for wine and other alcoholic drinks are included in many of the recipes.

First courses

First courses

The style of a first course is very important because it inevitably establishes the character of the ensuing meal. So sow the seeds of simple excellence right at the beginning and then build on them. A platter of mixed French, German and Italian salamis (allow about 2 oz/55 g per person), some olives and walnuts, and a loaf of freshly baked bread makes a fine opening for any meal and is very little trouble. First courses are opportunities too for enjoying morsels of luxury foods, asparagus (see p. 96 for cooking instructions), smoked cod's roe (about 2–3 oz/55–85 g per person) or smoked salmon (see p. 19) cannot fail to please.

With just a little more effort, many other simple first courses can be assembled. The following recipes are mostly for cold concoctions, avoiding the problem of cooking and timing successfully two hot courses.

AVOCADO AND CREAM CHEESE DIP

Avocado pears are rich in oils and protein and thus extremely nutritious. (Incidentally my health visitor tells me that it is one of the first solid foods small babies can eat.)

The avocados for sale in British shops are either the smooth-skinned green variety or the knobbly, very deep purple-brown kind but the criteria for selecting a good ripe one are the same. The pear should 'give' just a little when pressed by a finger or thumb around its apex, but it should have no very soft spots indicating that it has been bruised at some time. Often it's best to buy them slightly on the unripe side, when they damage less readily, and let them mature in a warm place at home.

Serve this dip with sticks of raw carrot or chicory leaves, and a loaf of brown bread. If you prepare the dip in advance, be sure to cover it because avocado browns if exposed to the air.

Preparation time: 5–10 minutes

For Six Helpings:
1 avocado
4 oz/115 g cream cheese
½ tsp salt
black pepper
pinch of cayenne pepper

1 Peel the avocado, remove the stone and mash the flesh.
2 Stir in the cream cheese, salt and black pepper.
3 Sprinkle the cayenne pepper over the dip.

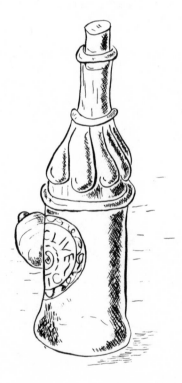

PRAWN AND RICE SALAD

Water chestnuts are the magic ingredients in this cold first course. Serve some chilled white wine, perhaps with a little sparkle in it, such as Portuguese Vinho Verde with the salad.

Preparation time: 10–15 minutes

For Six Helpings:
6 oz/170 g shelled prawns (or 14 oz/395 g unshelled prawns)
6 oz/170 g water chestnuts (sold in tins)
3 oz/85 g walnut pieces or blanched split almonds
1 lb/455 g cold cooked white rice (i.e.
    5–6 oz/140–170 g raw rice boiled in
    plenty of salted water for 10 minutes, drained
    and cooled)
1 large green pepper
1½ tsp salt
pepper

FOR THE DRESSING:
6 tbs olive oil
2 tbs lemon/lime juice

1   Remove the seeds from the pepper and chop it up roughly.
2   Slice the water chestnuts in half so that each gives you two discs. Peel the prawns if necessary.
3   Mix the olive oil and lemon juice together in the bottom of a serving bowl.
4   Heap the rice, pepper, prawns, water chestnuts, walnuts and seasoning into the bowl and toss together.

SMOKED SALMON THAI STYLE

The fresh coriander gives a pleasant piquancy to this luscious fish. Wafer-thin slices of buttered brown bread and wedges of lemon are the traditional accompaniments, and to drink serve an austere sherry or some still, or sparkling, dry white wine.

Preparation time: 5–10 minutes

For Six Helpings:
12–18 oz/340–510 g smoked salmon
2 tbs chopped fresh coriander leaves
pepper
12 lettuce leaves

1   Wash the lettuce and arrange it around the edge of a large plate.
2   Lay the smoked salmon in the centre of the dish and scatter over the fresh coriander and plenty of pepper.

GLOBE ARTICHOKES WITH MELTED BUTTER

These are delicious and an excellent excuse for enjoying some melted butter. They are available most of the year and are best when they are the size of small oranges and the tips of the petals on the globe (really a flower) are green, not brown.

The first time I was given an artichoke to eat, I was filled with dismay: was there any food on the object and how should I find it? I unravelled my napkin very slowly, took a long drink of water and watched my hosts' deft finger movements. So you need not suffer similarly, let me reveal that you begin by plucking the leaves from the globe and sucking their soft bases, and when all these have gone, you remove the needle-like choke and consume the tender and delicious heart.

Be sure to have several empty plates or bowls handy onto which the used leaves can be discarded. Incidentally globe artichokes are very easy to grow, and their spiky foliage is quite splendid.

Preparation time: 5–10 minutes
Cooking time: 40–55 minutes

For Six Helpings:
6 globe artichokes
3 pt/1.7 l water or sufficient to half cover them
3 tsp salt
4 oz/115 g butter
pepper

1 Set the salted water on to boil.
2 Cut the stalks from the artichokes, wash them and when the water reaches the boil put them in it with the globes facing uppermost.
3 Let the artichokes simmer for 40–55 minutes. They are cooked when you can easily remove a leaf from the globe. The exact time will depend on the size and age of the artichokes.
4 Just before the globes are cooked, melt the butter with some ground pepper in a small pan. Set a globe on each plate, and by its side make a pool of butter.

SALAD MIRANDA

Here is a recipe for a winter or summer salad you can serve either as a first course or, because it contains quite a bit of protein, as a light main dish. Bread and butter or baked potatoes make a good accompaniment, and, to drink, choose a light red or white wine.

You can keep the undressed salad quite well in the fridge for up to a couple of hours but if you do this don't add the prawns until the last minute as their flavour tends to pervade the others. It would also be a good idea to mix the dressing in a separate small dish so that the bottom of the salad doesn't go soggy while it's standing.

Preparation time: 15–20 minutes

For Six Helpings:

4 oz/115 g shelled prawns or 10 oz/285 g unpeeled prawns
1 flat lettuce or ½ Webbs or cos lettuce
4 oz/115 g watercress (i.e. about 1 bunch)
4 oz/115 g mange-touts – if they are not absolutely fresh, you will need to cook them (see notes on vegetables), otherwise they are nice raw in the salad
2 ripe avocados
⅓ of a cucumber
2 oz/55 g sliced cooked ham
2 oz/55 g thickly sliced spicy salami, peeled
1 tsp salt
pepper

FOR THE DRESSING:
¼ pt/140 ml olive oil
1½ tbs lemon/lime juice
½ tsp French mustard
1 tsp dill weed
½ tsp salt
pepper

1 If you have bought whole prawns, shell these first and set them on one side.

2 Next remove any fat from the ham and slice it, and the salami, into small pieces.
3 Remove the outer leaves from the lettuce and then wash the remainder and dry. Tear the big leaves in half.
4 Cut the stalks from the watercress.
5 Top and tail the mange-touts and peel the strings from their sides if they want to come away. Wash and dry them.
6 Peel the cucumber if you like it this way and then slice in to slivers.
7 Halve, stone and peel the avocados and then slice them up – a slippery job.
8 In the bottom of the salad bowl mix the olive oil, citric juice, mustard, dill, salt and pepper. Taste the dressing and adjust the seasoning if necessary.
9 Now put all the prepared ingredients in the bowl, add the seasoning, and toss the salad.

This is a dish to experiment with; if you don't care for some of the ingredients, try substituting something else. For example, you might prefer to use a few heads of chicory rather than lettuce or you could try a small pot of lumpfish roe (red or black – both are inexpensive). You could try adding some tomatoes.

The only thing not to change is the oil: it's fatal to use anything other than first pressing (virgin) olive oil. If you don't believe me, try it and I'll be surprised if you can't detect how infinitely superior is the taste of good olive oil.

GOATS' CHEESE TOASTS

Serve your guests these toasts piping hot from the oven and with them enjoy some bold, fairly young red wine (such as Beaujolais or Rioja) or white (say Frascati or Muscadet) or sherry. Steps 2–8 can be carried out in advance, and the sauce mixture will keep well in the fridge for several days.

Preparation time: 10–15 minutes
Cooking time: 15–20 minutes

For Six Helpings:
1 oz/30 g butter
1 clove of garlic
1 heaped tbs plain flour
¼ pt/140 ml single cream
2 oz/55 g moderate strength goats' cheese
1 egg yolk
¼–½ tsp salt
pepper
6 thick slices of white bread
optional: lettuce leaves or sprigs of watercress for garnishing

1 Set the oven to gas number 6 (400°F, 205°C).
2 Peel and chop the garlic.
3 Remove the rind from the cheese and chop it roughly.
4 Melt the butter in a saucepan and add the garlic. Cover the pan, and cook the garlic for a minute or two but on no account let the butter brown. Add the flour and mix in to form a roux.
5 Start to add the cream to the roux. Pour in only a very little at first – say a tablespoonful; mix it in well and then slowly add more, beating well in between each addition so you achieve a smooth paste. The sauce will be very thick. (If it is lumpy, put it through a sieve.)
6 When all the cream has been added, bring the sauce briefly to the boil and then stir in the goats' cheese and beat well. Taste the mixture and season accordingly.
7 Away from the heat, beat in the egg yolk rapidly.
8 Cut the slices of bread in half diagonally to form triangles (there's no need to remove the crusts) and on each spread a generous layer of the yellow mixture.
9 Put the bread pieces on a baking tray and slide into the top of the oven. Leave them to cook for 10–12 minutes. They are ready when the top of the paste has a suggestion of crispiness and the bread looks golden brown.
10 Remove the toasts from the oven and give each person two triangles. Garnish with the greenery if you have some.

VARIATIONS
You might like to try replacing the goats' cheese with: 2 heaped tbs pesto (basil) sauce or 1 dsp anchovy paste (and remember to omit the extra salt from the sauce mixture above).

A platter of mixed toasts: goats' cheese, basil and anchovy, or a pair of any of these, gives a tasty variety – and looks colourful.

SPICY SNACKS

These are good appetite-ticklers; beer or wine goes well with them. They keep well for several days in an air-tight tin.

Preparation time: 15–20 minutes
Cooking time: 10 minutes
Cooling time: 30 minutes

For about 35–40 biscuits:
2 oz/55 g butter at room temperature
4 oz/115 g plain flour
3 level dsp grated Parmesan cheese
½ tsp salt
1 tsp hot curry powder
½ tsp ground coriander
½ tsp allspice
½ tsp garam masala
sprinkle of ground cinnamon
pepper
1 egg yolk
2 dsp cold water
1 heaped dsp poppy seed
a couple of tbs of flour for the rolling out
nob of butter

1 Set the oven to Reg. 6 (400°F, 205°C).
2 Grease a large baking tin with the nob of butter.
3 Put the flour in a bowl and add the butter, cut up in small pieces.
4 With your fingers gently rub the butter into the flour so that it goes into tinier and tinier bits, eventually blending with the flour completely. Test to see whether this has been achieved, by shaking the bowl for a second or two. The butterfat pieces, if there are any left, will rise to the surface.
5 Add the cheese, salt, curry powder, coriander, allspice, garam masala, cinnamon and pepper and stir in.
6 Drop the egg yolk into the flour mixture and add the water. Now gently mix the liquids in to bind together. After a few moments the mixture should hold together in a ball.
7 Scatter the other flour over a flat surface and onto it put the biscuit mixture and roll it around gently so it becomes coated with flour.
8 Roll out the mixture to about ⅛ inch/0.25 cm thick.
9 Use a pastry-cutter, sharp knife or rim of a glass to cut the sheet of pastry into pieces a bit larger than 50ps. Lay them in the baking tin.
10 Scatter the poppy seeds over the biscuits and transfer them to the middle of the oven for 10 minutes. They are ready when they are a pale golden colour beneath their poppy coat.
11 Remove the snacks from the oven and use a spatula knife to lift them to cool and dry on a wire rack for about half an hour.

EGG AND ANCHOVY RAMEKINS

Here is a hot first course of eggs cooked with a little cream and some chopped anchovy fillet.

You will need six little ramekin pots.

Preparation time: 10–15 minutes
Cooking time: 12–14 minutes

For Six Helpings:
6 eggs
9 anchovy fillets (i.e. a tin)
6 tbs single cream
freshly ground pepper
brown or white bread for toast
a sprig or two of parsley for garnishing
nob of butter for greasing the dishes

1   Set the oven to Reg. 5 (375°F, 190°C).
2   Lightly smear the butter over the pots.
3   Break an egg into each pot, and over it grind some pepper. (Sufficient salt will be provided by the anchovies.) Give each egg one tbs of cream.
4   Cut each of the fillets into about four pieces and sprinkle 1½ fillets' worth over each egg.
5   Put the pots in the top part of the oven and let them cook for 12 minutes.
6   Remove the stalks from the parsley and sort it into little florets. Make the toast.
7   By now the 12 minutes will probably be up; the egg white should be just firm, and a white veil should have covered the yolk. If, on testing the white (don't puncture the yolk to test it), it still seems liquid, give the ramekins a minute or two more.
8   Remove the pots from the oven immediately they are ready; scatter over a little parsley and serve at once with toast.

KIPPER PÂTÉ

Pâtés are very useful because you can either serve them as a first course at table or hand them round before sitting down – and they go well with almost any kind of wine, aperitif or beer. This pâté is soft and creamy so it needs to be spread on toast.

This is much less rich than smoked mackerel pâté and very easy to make. It will keep well in the fridge for several days.

Preparation time: 10–15 minutes

For Six Helpings:
8 oz/225 g kipper fillets
2 tbs single cream
juice of ½ lemon
freshly ground black pepper

1   Peel the skins from the fillets and remove any stray bones from the flesh.
2   Chop the fillets roughly and then put them with the lemon juice, cream and a good grinding of pepper (but no salt) in a blender or food processor and turn to a purée.

CHICKEN LIVER PÂTÉ

I have made this recipe for years and have never known it to fail. It can be prepared a day in advance and will keep well in the fridge for two to three days, but then it will begin to lose its freshness and acquires a kind of stale-fridge taste.

Preparation time: 15–20 minutes
Cooking time: not more than 10 minutes
Cooling time: 2 hours

For Six Helpings:
½ medium-sized onion
3 cloves of garlic
8 oz/225 g chicken livers
4 oz/115 g butter
1 tsp salt
pepper
1 tsp dried basil
2 tbs brandy
slices of brown or white bread for toasting

1 Peel and chop the onion. Peel and chop the garlic finely.
2 Pick over the chicken livers and remove any white, stringy-looking bits. Cut each liver into about four or five pieces.
3 Take 1 oz/30 g of butter and melt it in a saucepan. Add the onion and garlic and cook for a minute together – do not let them brown.
4 Add the livers, basil and seasoning and stir together.
5 Cover the pan and let the livers cook for 5 to 8 minutes, when drops of blood should come to their surface and they are pale pink inside if cut with a knife.
6 Transfer the liver mixture to a food processor or liquidizer, add the remaining butter (the hot livers will melt it) and brandy, and blend to a smooth paste.
7 Taste and check the seasoning and when you are satisfied with it pour the mixture into a small pot suitable for serving from later, and cover.
8 Set the pâté in the fridge for at least a couple of hours to cool and mature.
9 Toast some bread and serve it with the pâté.

QUICHE LORRAINE

I hope you have not been prejudiced against this tart by the poor substitute, so often found in Britain, of wedges of solid egg custard dotted with bacon lying in a thick pastry shell. I suppose our desire to eat protein, rather than calorific pastry, has encouraged the evolution of these miserable mimics but by so doing the point of the quiche has been lost. A thin layer of creamy savoury custard should paint a crisp shell so that you are left with a feeling of having consumed something buttery and delicate, not a lead balloon.

Preparation time: 20–25 minutes
Cooking time: 30 minutes

For Six to Eight Helpings:
FOR THE PASTRY:
8 oz/225 g plain flour
4 oz/115 g butter (at room temperature so it's soft)
½ tsp salt
2½ tbs cold water
nob of butter for greasing the tin
a few tbs flour to roll the pastry out on

FOR THE FILLING:
1 leek
4 oz/115 g back bacon
½ oz/15 g butter
3 eggs
½ pt/285 ml single cream
pepper
½ tsp salt

1 Set the oven to Reg. 6 (400°F, 205°C).
2 First prepare the filling. Break the eggs into a mixing bowl and whisk them up with the cream, salt and some pepper.
3 Remove the outer leaf from the leek and then slice it into wafer-thin discs. Wash them.

4 Remove the rind from the bacon and cut it up into pieces the size of cocktail biscuits.
5 Melt the butter in a frying pan and add the leek and bacon. Fry together for about 5 minutes so that the bacon becomes pale pink and the leeks soft.
6 Add the bacon and leek mixture to the eggs and cream and whisk together.
7 Grease the sides and bottom of a flan tin (about 11 inches/28 cm in diameter) with the butter.
8 Put the flour, salt and butter in a mixing bowl. With a sharp knife cut the butter into small pieces and then let your fingers take over and rub the fat between them so that the butter is reduced to tinier and tinier particles that eventually mix with the flour completely. Check to see this has been achieved by shaking the bowl and observing whether any pieces of butter rise to the surface; if they do, rub them in.
9 Add the cold water and work it in with your hands so that, after about a minute, the pastry holds together in a ball. Add a little more water if need be.
10 Sprinkle the flour on a clean surface over an area a bit larger than the size of the tin.
11 Put the pastry on the floured surface and, rubbing a little flour over a rolling-pin, roll the pastry out. Make the first roll away from you and then turn the pastry through a right-angle and repeat the stroke. Now you should have a fairly rectangular piece of pastry to roll out to a little larger than the size of your tin. Be careful all the time to see that there is plenty of flour under the pastry so that it doesn't stick to the surface.
12 When the pastry sheet is the correct size, wrap it very gently around the rolling-pin so you can transfer it to the tin.
13 Lay the pastry in the tin and press the base gently in place. The sides will probably have fallen into

the middle, so mould them against the sides of the tin, making sure there is plenty of pastry to take the bend between the base and the upright sides and dangle over the edge. (The pastry will contract as it cooks, and if you wish, you can remove the excess after the cooking.)

4 Prick the bottom of the pastry in a couple of places and then put it in the top of the oven for 5 minutes.

5 Remove the partially cooked pastry shell from the oven. Turn the oven down to Reg. 4 (350°F, 175°C).

6 Pat down the centre of the pastry shell if it has puffed up. (Sometimes the sides fall in: when this happens, gently coax the soft pastry back into position and reinforce it with trimmings left over from the rolling-out.)

7 Pour the filling mixture into the shell and return the tin to the oven. Let it cook there for 20 minutes. By this time the egg custard should just have set, and the top will have puffed up and browned. It will sink as it cools.

MUSHROOM QUICHE

There are many possible variations on the basic quiche mixture. Here is just one.

Preparation time: 20–25 minutes
Cooking time: 30 minutes

Ingredients are the same as for Quiche Lorraine (for 6–8 helpings) except substitute ½ lb/225 g mushrooms for the bacon, use half an onion instead of the leek and add ¼ tsp grated nutmeg.

1–2 As Quiche Lorraine.
3 Peel the mushrooms and remove the stalks if you wish. Slice into slivers.
4 Peel and chop the onion finely.
5 Melt the butter in a pan and to it add the onion and mushrooms. Fry gently together for about 5 minutes until the mushroom slivers and onion are just soft.
6 Add the mushrooms and onion to the egg and cream mixture and stir in the nutmeg.
7–17 Continue as for Quiche Lorraine.

Here are some other ideas for first courses:

Watercress omelette (see p. 91)
Chicken livers with dill (see p. 60)
Tagliatelle with mushrooms (see p. 78)
Pasta with fish and basil (see p. 76)
Cucumber and avocado salad (see p. 103)
Salad of pasta (see p. 104)

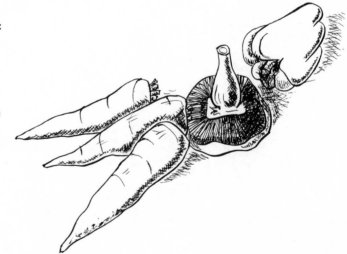

Soups

Soups

There are two kinds of recipes in this chapter: soups that are the centre of a simple lunch or supper, and those that are eaten at the beginning of a grander meal. Into the first group go those that are fairly nutritious, such as bacon and lentil soup, fish soup and Oriental broth; the veal and pea, spinach and coconut, and chilled tomato and coriander soups are lighter and therefore better served before some meat or fish.

  None of the following recipes requires stocks – home-made or the stock-cube variety. Each of these has its disadvantages: home-made stocks take several hours of supervision to prepare, and the ones you can make up from the cubes tend to have a drab quality which they impart to the soups. The way to overcome this problem is to include a little protein in the soups, and this gives them their 'body', as would a home-made stock.

BACON AND LENTIL SOUP

A hearty, warming soup for the winter – or British summer. The soup can be re-heated very easily and can be made with great success the day before it is needed.

Preparation time: 10–15 minutes
Cooking time: 50–60 minutes

For Six to Eight Helpings:
1 lb/455 g orange split dried lentils
½ lb/225 g sliced lean (back) bacon
2 onions (only 1 if they are large)
2 carrots
3 pt/1.7 l water
2 tbs olive oil
1 heaped tsp ground cumin
2 tsp salt
pepper
optional: **milk**

1   Peel and chop the onions and carrots.
2   Cut up the bacon into small pieces, discarding some of the fat if you wish.
3   Pour the oil into a large saucepan and when it is warm add the vegetables and diced bacon and cook for a couple of minutes over a moderate flame. Do not let them brown.
4   Add the lentils, seasoning, spice and water.
5   Bring the mixture to the boil, stirring regularly; cover and let it simmer gently for three-quarters of an hour. Look at it from time to time to ensure that it isn't burning on the bottom of the pan.
6   It is ready when the lentils have become soft and have broken up to give a thickish soup. Stir it to see whether it will form a thick, homogeneous mass. If you are doubtful, cook the soup for another 10 minutes. Taste and adjust the seasoning if necessary. (If the soup is too thick for your liking, add a little milk.)

FISH SOUP

This requires a little more preparation but is well worth the trouble. Steps 1–5 can be carried out in advance but do try to avoid re-heating the soup after the fish has been added because fish spoils so easily with too much cooking.

Preparation time: 15–20 minutes
Cooking time: 20–25 minutes

For Six Helpings:
1 lb/455 g smoked haddock fillets
10 oz/285 g unshelled prawns, or 4 oz/110 g shelled
    prawns
1 onion
1½ lb/680 g potatoes
1 green pepper
2 fresh green chillis
1 oz/30 g butter
1 heaped dsp flour
2 pt/1.1 l water
1 bay leaf
1 tsp salt
pepper
½ pt/285 ml single cream (or milk for a less rich
    soup)

1 Peel and chop the onion finely. Peel the potatoes and dice them, and the pepper, into 20p-size pieces.
2 Remove the seeds from the chillis under running water and chop up very finely.
3 Melt the butter in a large saucepan and add the diced onion, potato, pepper and chilli. Let them fry for a few minutes but on no account let the vegetables brown.
4 Add the water, bay leaf and seasoning, and bring the broth to the boil; simmer gently for 10 minutes.
5 While the vegetables are cooking, prepare the fish. To remove the skin from the fish hold a fillet, skin side down, on a table or board with your left hand, and with your right hand scrape off the flesh with the knife by sliding it down between two layers of muscle, so that it just touches the underlying skin, and then cutting the flesh away. It is easiest to go with the grain of the fish and to direct your cutting and sliding motions away from your body. Repeat the operation on each fillet in turn. Remove any odd bones and cut the fish into pieces the size of 50p coins. Shell the prawns.
6 Add the fish and prawns to the vegetable stock, return to the boil and let the concoction simmer for a further 10 minutes.
7 Pour in the cream (or milk), taste and adjust the seasoning if necessary.

ORIENTAL BROTH

This is the kind of soup I have seen people eating for breakfast, or lunch, in Thailand. The dash of sesame oil, which is added just before serving, gives the soup a mysterious delicacy.

Steps 1–5 can be carried out in advance.

Preparation time: 10–15 minutes
Cooking time: 15–20 minutes

For Six Helpings:
4 tbs peanut (or olive) oil
4 cloves garlic
1 onion
2 oz/55 g fresh ginger root
4 oz/115 g mushrooms
8 oz/225 g chicken breast
8 oz/225 g bean sprouts
2 heads chicory
3 tsp salt
2½ pt/1.4 l water
½ tsp sesame oil

1 Peel and chop the garlic and onion finely. Peel the ginger and grate it up (be careful of your fingers). Peel, or wash, the mushrooms, remove their stalks (if you wish) and slice them roughly.
2 Dice the chicken into small nuggets the size of 20p coins.
3 Melt the oil in a large saucepan and into it throw the garlic, onion, ginger and mushrooms. Let them fry for a couple of minutes but do not let them brown.
4 Stir in the chicken, seasoning and water and bring to the boil. Cover the pot and let the soup simmer gently for 15 minutes.
5 While the broth is cooking, chop up the bean sprouts so they will fit in a soup spoon. Remove the outer leaves from the chicory and slice it up too.
6 Add the bean sprouts and chicory to the broth and cook for another minute. Just before serving, stir in the sesame oil.

VARIATION
Vegetarians might like to replace the chicken with bean curd. Chop it into small cubes and add it with the bean sprouts and chicory in step 6.

VEAL AND PEA SOUP

Serve this soup with brown bread and butter, or perhaps a loaf of garlic bread.

Steps 1–6 may be carried out in advance.

Preparation time: 15–20 minutes
Cooking time: 15–20 minutes

For Six Helpings:
8 oz/225 g lean veal
1 onion (or 2 leeks)
2 tbs olive oil
1½ lb/680 g peas in their pods or about 12 oz/340 g
    frozen peas
2½ pt/1.4 l water
3 tsp salt
pepper
4 sprigs fresh mint or 1½ tsp dried mint leaves

1   Peel and chop the onion finely.
2   Remove any fat from the meat and then dice it up finely too.
3   Pour the olive oil into a large pot and to it add the onion and veal. Cook slowly for a few minutes but do not let them become brown.
4   Add the water and seasoning and set the broth to simmer gently for 15 minutes.
5   Pod the peas.
6   If you are using fresh mint, chop up the leaves roughly.
7   Add the peas and mint to the soup and simmer for a further 3–4 minutes to cook the peas.
8   Taste the soup and adjust the seasoning if necessary.

VARIATION
Vegetarians might like this soup without the veal.

SPINACH AND COCONUT SOUP

This soup gets its 'body' from coconut milk, which is fairly nutritious. It can be served either hot or cold, with brown bread and butter.

Preparation time: 15–20 minutes
Cooking time: 10–15 minutes
(Chilling time: at least 4 hours)

For Six to Seven Helpings:
2 lb/905 g fresh raw spinach or about 30 oz/850 g
    frozen chopped spinach
1 onion
2 cloves of garlic
2 tbs peanut oil
1 heaped tsp garam masala
1 heaped tbs flour
1 pt/570 ml thin coconut milk*
1 pt/570 ml water
3 level tsp salt
pepper

1   Your first task is to prepare the fresh spinach. Wash it, remove the stalks and put the wet spinach straight into a large pan or wok. Bring it to the boil and let it simmer for 5 minutes. Transfer it, and its cooking liquid, to a large bowl.
2   Peel and chop the onion and garlic finely.
3   Pour the oil into a large saucepan and slide in the onion and garlic. Add the spice. Fry together for a few minutes.
4   Stir in the flour. Add the coconut milk, water, spinach (and its cooking liquid) and seasoning.
5   Simmer the mixture for 10 minutes and then purée it.
6   Either return the purée to a pan to re-heat it for serving or put it in the fridge to chill for 4 hours or overnight.

*   To make the thin coconut milk, mix 4 oz/110 g creamed coconut or 2 oz/55 g coconut cream powder with 1 pt/570 ml hot water.

CHILLED TOMATO AND CORIANDER SOUP

I developed this soup from the famous Spanish gazpacho of tomatoes, peppers, garlic and cucumber. This is an aromatic soup too, though here it comes from the piquancy of crushed coriander leaves. It requires no cooking. Serve the soup with brown bread and butter and, if possible, some dry, slightly bubbly white wine.

It will keep well in the fridge for several hours. If you want to make it a whole day in advance, I think it is better to wait to add the coriander (step 5) until a couple of hours before serving because its delicate character will be lost if it is left for too long in the tomato mixture.

Preparation time: 15–20 minutes
Chilling time: 1–2 hours

For Six to Seven Helpings:
2 oz/55 g white bread
4 tbs olive oil
3 lb/1.35 kg ripe tomatoes
2 cloves of garlic
1 level tbs salt
pepper
1 pt/570 ml ice-cold water
12 stems of fresh coriander leaves

1 Peel and chop the garlic roughly and then work your way through the tomatoes, washing and quartering them.
2 Put the bread in a liquidizer or food processor, add the olive oil and garlic and reduce the bread to crumbs.
3 Add the tomatoes, say a pound (half a kilo) at a time, to the mixer and blend together very thoroughly so they form a fine purée.
4 Turn the tomato mixture into a serving bowl and into it stir the cold water and the seasoning.
5 Chop the fresh coriander leaves finely. Stir the leaves into the soup, cover the bowl and put it in the fridge for a good hour to let the flavours ripen and amalgamate.

Fish

Fish

If trout, mackerel or any other whole fish slips through your hands as you try to slither it into a pan, it is fresh. If you want to be successful in cooking fish, it is essential to purchase fish that is, at the very most, not more than a day old and still wearing its slippery proteinaceous coat. This should not be difficult to achieve because fresh fish is now widely available throughout Britain in old-fashioned fishmonger shops, town markets and, more recently, supermarkets. Of course the advantage of purchasing fish from a fishmonger is that you can seek his knowledge and advice about which fish are in season, the quantities to buy, methods of preparation and cooking. If you ask to have the fish gutted, filleted or even skinned, he will probably oblige.

Fish needs to be cooked rapidly from room temperature so it is best to remove it from the fridge several hours before the cooking. Its flesh is far less dense than that of red meat, and so a piece of fish will cook much quicker than a piece of red meat of the same dimensions. Unlike meat, there is no obvious colour-change to gauge its progress but the texture of the flesh is a good indicator. Raw fish feels slightly sticky when a sharp knife is withdrawn from it; the cooked flesh is soft and yielding, and it should part from the main bones (such as a backbone) quite easily, but it should not all fall apart. Just as soon as it is ready, remove the fish from the heat: delays can spell disappointment precisely because it cooks so fast, and there will always be some residual heat in the fish which will prolong the cooking anyway. The perils of re-heating fish are legion, and it is best, if possible, to avoid it; nevertheless, much of the preliminary preparation can often be done in advance.

Most fish has a delicate flavour which should be treated with respect and not swamped by the flavour of accompanying vegetables, and it is for this reason that it is customary to serve simply prepared greenery rather than dishes loaded with garlic and spices. Most vegetables go well with fish, with the exception of the brassicas, the botanical family of cabbages which also include Brussels sprouts, cauliflower and broccoli, probably because of their characteristic slightly acrid flavour (which is due to the presence of mustard oils in their tissues).

BAKED TROUT

Fresh river trout requires only simple treatment. Boiled potatoes and carrots in a creamy dill sauce (see p. 99) go well with the fish, and so does a glass of dry white wine.

Preparation time: 5–10 minutes
Cooking time: 20–30 minutes

For Six Helpings:
6 gutted trout (ask the fishmonger to do this) each weighing 8–12 oz/225–340 g
2 oz/55 g butter
3 tsp salt
pepper
6 wedges of lemon
optional: **a few sprigs of parsley for garnishing the trout**

1   Set the oven to Reg. 5 (375°F, 190°C) and let it warm up for ten minutes.
2   Use a small amount of the butter to grease the inside of an ovenproof dish and then lay the trout in it. Sprinkle them with salt and a generous amount of pepper.
3   Cut the rest of the butter into sugarlump-sized pieces and scatter them over the fish.
4   Place a piece of foil over the dish and transfer it to the top part of the oven.
5   The trout will be cooked in 20–30 minutes, depending on their size. Serve the fish (garnished with parsley if you have it) with the slices of lemon.

VARIATIONS
A sprinkling of poppy, sesame or sunflower seeds or pine kernels over the fish before the cooking makes a pleasing alternative.

BAKED SALMON TROUT

I prefer the lighter flesh of salmon (or sea) trout to salmon itself, and they come in reasonable sizes for a whole fish to serve five or six people. It is an excellent fish, so do not mask it with complicated vegetables: fresh green beans, peas or mange-touts, and boiled potatoes are simple to prepare and the best background for the salmon trout, which may be served hot or cold. Dry white wine, from any country, is the drink for this sea feast.

Preparation time: 5–10 minutes
Cooking time: 35–45 minutes

For Five to Six Helpings:
1 salmon trout weighing about 2½ lb/1.1 kg (ask the fishmonger to gut it)
2 oz/55 g butter
3 tsp salt
pepper

1   Set the oven to Reg. 5 (375°F, 190°C) and let it warm up for ten minutes.
2   Wash the fish under running water, making sure that the blood vessel that runs down the inside of the fish has been broken and the blood washed away; if you don't do this, the flesh around it will go a rather unpleasant brown as it cooks.
3   Use about half the butter to grease (very generously) a piece of foil large enough to enclose the fish. Lay the fish on the foil, scatter over the seasoning and dot over the butter. Draw the two long sides of the foil together and fold them together neatly – so you will be able to undo them easily. Make each end fast.
4   Put the fish in the middle of the pre-heated oven and let it cook for about half an hour – that is, 10 minutes per pound (or half kilo) of fish.
5   At the end of this time, look to see whether it is

done. Unravel some of the foil and insert a sharp knife into the centre of one of the sides near the backbone. The skin may be a little tough but the flesh should just give as you penetrate it; if it feels slightly resistant and 'sticky', it is not ready, so return it to the oven and give it another 10 to 15 minutes and then test it again. (The cooking time will be longer if you began with a fridge-cold fish.)

6   Turn off the oven and leave the fish in it for a further 5–10 minutes to complete its cooking.
7   Unwrap the foil, slide the fish onto a serving dish and pour over its cooking juices.

VARIATION

If you have a fish kettle, simply put the fish, without any foil, on the buttered tray, add more fat and seasoning and let it simmer over a little water for 10 minutes per pound or half kilo. Let it sit for 5–10 minutes with the heat turned off to finish the cooking and then serve. (The cooking water should be discarded.)

GRILLED HERRINGS

These are excellent served on a bed of Genoan potatoes (see p. 101).

Preparation time: 5 minutes
Cooking time: 10–12 minutes

For Six Helpings:
6 herrings (gutted and heads removed if possible)
2 tsp salt
pepper

1   Turn the grill on to medium strength.
2   Gut the fish and chop off the heads if necessary.
3   Sprinkle half the seasoning over the fish and then put them under the grill for about ten minutes (turning them after five minutes).

HALIBUT WITH LIMES

Halibut is fairly rich and not as low in fat as some other kinds of fish; all the same, its firm flesh makes fine eating. Serve the hot cutlets with potatoes or rice and beans, or follow it with a green salad.

Preparation time: 5–10 minutes
Grilling time: 10 minutes

For Six Helpings:
6–8 oz/170–225 g halibut 'steaks'
3 tsp salt
pepper
3 limes

1 Turn the grill to its middle setting.
2 Wash the fish under cold water to remove any blood. Lay them in the grill tray (it is not necessary to coat with butter as they will release fat as they cook). Sprinkle over the salt and a hearty grinding of pepper.
3 Put the fish under the heat and leave them to cook for 10 minutes. They should not need turning because the heat will penetrate to their undersides and cook them.
4 Halve the limes.
5 At the end of 10 minutes test the fish to see whether they are cooked; if they are not, give them a few more minutes. Serve the grilled halibut with the wedges of lime.

HADDOCK WITH MINT SAUCE

This fish, which is caught in northern waters, has firm flesh and a delicate flavour. Buttered noodles or potatoes and some spinach are all this dish needs to show it to its best advantage. To drink, choose some dry white wine, or try it with Beaujolais for a change.

Steps 4–6 can be carried out in advance.

Preparation time: 10–15 minutes
Cooking time: 20–25 minutes

For Six Generous Helpings:
2½ lb/1.1 kg fresh (or frozen) haddock fillets (or substitute cod or whiting fillets)
1 oz/30 g butter
1 tsp salt
pepper

FOR THE SAUCE:
1 large onion
1 oz/30 g butter
6 sprigs fresh mint (or 2 dsp dried mint leaves)
½ pt/285 ml water
1 tsp salt
pepper
1 tbs dry sherry

1   Set the oven at Reg. 5 (375°F, 190°C).
2   Butter the bottom and sides of an ovenproof dish with a third of the butter and then lay the fish fillets in it. Apply salt and pepper and dot over the remaining butter.
3   Cut a piece of foil the area of the dish and rest it over the fish and then transfer it all to the middle of the oven for 20–25 minutes.
4   While the fish is cooking, prepare the sauce. First peel and chop the onion. Now melt the butter in a small saucepan and add the onion, salt and pepper.

Fry gently for 5 minutes but on no account let the onion and butter brown.
5   Next pour in the water, add the sherry and bring the sauce to the boil. Cover the pan and let the sauce simmer for 10–15 minutes over a gentle heat.
6   If you are using fresh mint, remove the leaves from the stalks, discarding any bad ones, and chop the leaves up finely. Set on one side.
7   Test to see if the fish is cooked; when it is, add the mint to the sauce, stir it in and serve it with the haddock.

GRILLED MACKEREL WITH LEEKS AND WATERCRESS

In this dish the watercress and leeks counterbalance the rich nature of mackerel. Eat the fish with potatoes or thick slices of bread and butter, and afterwards serve a simple green salad. Beer, cider or wine goes equally well with mackerel cooked in this manner.

Preparation time: 10–15 minutes
Cooking time: 10 minutes

For Six Helpings:
6 mackerel (ask the fishmonger to gut them and remove their heads)
3 tsp salt
pepper

FOR THE SAUCE:
1 lb/455 g leeks
1½ oz/40 g butter
1 tsp salt
pepper
3 tbs water
8 oz/225 g (2 bunches) of watercress
¼ pt/140 ml single cream

1 Turn the grill onto medium strength.
2 Top and tail the leeks, slice into thin discs (as thick as 50p pieces) and wash them.
3 Wash the fish thoroughly. Make three incisions across the bodies of the fish on each side (to help prevent the skins from bursting, and make them look attractive for serving).
4 Set the mackerel on the grill tray (it is not necessary to grease it, as the fish will release fat during the cooking); scatter over half the salt and plenty of pepper and set the fish under the grill for 5–6 minutes, when you will need to turn them over (see step 8).
5 Melt the butter in a pan and to it add the leeks. Fry together for a couple of minutes but do not let the butter or leeks brown.
6 Add the water, salt and pepper, cover the pan and let the leeks gently sauté for 8–10 minutes.
7 Remove the stems from the watercress.
8 Inspect the fish after 5 minutes, and if their top sides look slightly crisp and brown, turn them all over and put them under the heat once more for another five minutes. (They will keep quite happily under the hot turned-off grill while you finish off the sauce.)
9 When the leeks are tender, add the watercress. Pour on the cream, bring it to the boil and heap the sauce over the fish.

HUMBLE PIE

Not a grand dish, but a heart-warming supper for a cosy party. Unlike other fish dishes, cabbage goes well with the pie, and so do baked potatoes, or just follow it with a green salad. To drink serve beer or red or white wine.

The pie may be assembled in advance of the cooking but if you do this, allow the sauce to cool a little before pouring it over the fish – so you don't cook it – and add an extra 5–10 minutes to the cooking time to allow the sauce to warm up.

Preparation time: 15–20 minutes
Cooking time: 55–65 minutes

For Six Generous Helpings:
2 lb/905 g cod fillets (skinned if possible)
1 pt/570 ml cockles (fresh, not vinegared)
2 leeks
2 oz/55 g walnut pieces
1 tsp salt
freshly ground pepper
4 oz/115 g white bread to make into breadcrumbs
½ oz/15 g butter

FOR THE SAUCE:
3 oz/85 g butter
2½ oz/70 g flour
1¼ pt/710 ml milk
1 tsp salt
freshly ground pepper

1 Set the oven to Reg. 4 (350°F, 175°C).
2 Make the breadcrumbs, grating the bread or using a food processor.
3 Use a little of the butter to grease the inside of a large pie dish.
4 Wash the fish and then, if the fishmonger has not removed the skin from the cod fillets, do this. Hold the fish flat on a surface, skin side down, with one hand and with the other use a knife to separate the flesh from the skin. Cut through the flesh down to the skin and then ease the flesh away as you draw the knife under it. Repeat this operation with the other bits of cod. Remove any stray bones.
5 Cut the skinned cod into pieces the size of small potatoes and then divide the fish into two piles.
6 Wash the cockles.
7 Wash, top and tail the leeks and remove their outer layer; then slice into 50 p-thick discs.
8 Now melt the butter in a pan and to it add the sliced leeks. Let them sauté gently for 5 minutes. Tip in the flour and stir it in.
9 Slowly, very slowly at first, start adding the milk to the butter-and-flour roux. Beat it well in between each addition so that you form a smooth, lump-free sauce. Continue with the rest of the liquid and bring it to the boil. Then add the seasoning, taste the sauce and add more salt or pepper according to your liking. The sauce should be very thick.
10 Now you can put the pie together. Arrange half the cod in the bottom of the pie dish and sprinkle on a little salt and pepper.
11 Now the cockles and then the walnuts go in. Season a little more.
12 Pour on the leek sauce.
13 Lay the rest of the cod in the dish and over it sprinkle the last of the seasoning. Spread over the breadcrumbs and dot the surface with pieces of butter.
14 Leave the pie to cook in the middle of the oven for about ¾ hour. At the end of this time the breadcrumbs should be nicely browned and the fish tender.

PRAWN AND CABBAGE RAGOÛT

This recipe uses Oriental spices but its real secret is freshness: it should be served as soon as it is cooked because the prawns will lose their character if kept hot for long. Serve the ragoût with rice noodles or rice and wash it down with beer or lager.

Steps 1–5 can be done in advance.

Preparation time: 15–20 minutes
Cooking time: about 10 minutes

For Six Good Helpings:
1 green/white cabbage weighing about 2 lb/905 g
2¼ lb/1 kg unpeeled prawns or 1 lb/455 g peeled
   prawns (frozen prawns take about 1–1½ hours
   to thaw)
2 green peppers
1lb/455 g mushrooms
4 cloves garlic
2 oz/55 g fresh ginger root
4 tbs peanut oil
2–3 tsp salt
pepper

1 If you have bought unpeeled prawns, shelling them is your first task.
2 Wash or peel the mushrooms, remove the stalks (if you wish) and slice them up. Quarter and core the peppers and chop them up. Peel the garlic and chop it up finely. Peel and grate the ginger.
3 Next prepare the cabbage by peeling off the outer leaves, halving and then quartering, removing the core and then slicing it into manageable pieces. Wash it.
4 Measure the oil into a large saucepan or casserole, set over a moderate heat and add the garlic and ginger. Fry for a minute. Then add the mushrooms, cabbage and pepper and fry the mixture for a few more minutes.
5 Now add the prawns and some seasoning, cover the pan and let it all cook for 10 minutes. (The prawns should exude some juice as they cook, so there is no need to add any.)
6 Test to see whether the vegetables are cooked; they should retain a little crispness. Taste and adjust the seasoning if necessary.

GRATIN OF COD

This is an excellent dish for a cold winter's evening. Rice or baked potatoes and carrots make good accompaniments.

The fish and sauce can be prepared ahead of the final cooking. If you wish to do this, allow the sauce to cool before pouring it over the fish (otherwise you will cook the flesh) and later allow an extra 5–10 minutes in the baking because all the ingredients will be cold.

Preparation time: 15–20 minutes
Cooking time: 35–40 minutes

For Six Helpings:
2½–3 lb/1.1–1.35 kg fresh (or frozen) cod (or haddock or whiting) fillets (ask the fishmonger to skin them)
½ oz/15 g butter
1 tsp salt
pepper
2 oz/55 g stoned black or green olives

FOR THE SAUCE:
3 oz/85 g butter
2½ oz/70 g plain flour
1¼ pt/710 ml milk
3 oz/85 g Cheddar or other sharp cheese
3 oz/85 g Gruyère or Emmenthal cheese
pinch nutmeg
1 tsp salt
pepper

1 Set the oven at Reg. 5 (375°F, 190°C).
2 Butter the bottom and sides of a large ovenproof dish.
3 Wash the fish, shake off the water and, if they have not been skinned, do this. Hold the fish flat on a surface, skin side down, with one hand and with the other use a knife to separate the flesh from the skin. Cut through the flesh down to the skin and then ease the flesh away as you draw the knife under it. Repeat this operation with the other bits of cod. Then put the fillets in the dish and sprinkle on salt and pepper.
4 Now grate the cheese, keeping the two varieties separate.
5 Melt the butter in a saucepan over a gentle heat, making sure it does not brown. Add the flour and stir it in. Cook for a minute. Now start adding the milk very slowly so that you form a paste at first, then a smooth sauce. (If it is lumpy, put it through a sieve.)
6 When all the liquid has been added, stir in the Cheddar cheese, nutmeg and salt and pepper it to taste. Bring it to the boil briefly. Then pour it over the fish and scatter on the Swiss cheese.
7 Transfer the dish to the top part of the oven for half an hour, when the fish should be tender and the surface of the gratin brown and bubbling.
8 Just before serving, sprinkle over the olives.

SQUID CURRY

Serve this creamy curry with plenty of boiled rice and afterwards a dish of beans or a salad. Very dry white wine goes well with the dish.

Preparation time: 10–15 minutes
Cooking time: 20–25 minutes

For Six Helpings:
4½ lb/2 kg squid (prepared if possible by the fishmonger)
3–4 fresh green chillis
3 cloves garlic
2 tbs olive or peanut oil
3 tbs dry sherry
1–1½ tsp salt
pepper
¼ pt/140 ml single cream
2 oz/55 g grated Parmesan cheese

1   If the fishmonger has not prepared the squid this is your first task. Wash the squid thoroughly and remove the heads (but keep the tentacles because these are edible) and the attached viscera from the inside of their bodies. There is also a cellophane-like strip, and this needs to be pulled out too. You should be left with a sac rather like a floppy ice-cream cone.
2   Slice the squid into half-inch (1 cm) thick rings.
3   Peel and chop the garlic finely. Remove the seeds from the chillis under running water and chop them up very finely.
4   Pour the oil into a large frying-pan or wok and fry the garlic and chilli for a minute.
5   Add the squid (rings and tentacles), salt and pepper, toss together and then cover the pan (use silver foil if it doesn't have a lid) and let the squid cook over a moderate heat for about 20 minutes. Give it a stir occasionally.
6   Pour in the cream and dry sherry and then stir in the Parmesan cheese.

Meat

Meat

There is one major decision to make when you decide to cook meat: a joint or a casserole? The former is much simpler to cook because all that is needed is to sit the piece of meat in a roasting tin, season and slip it into a hot oven. Nevertheless, it can be quite difficult mastering the timing of the operations so that all the vegetables, sauces and other accompaniments are ready simultaneously. The alternative of preparing a casserole is generally less expensive, if you do not count your time. The cooking is longer but it does not require such fine tuning, though stews can be cooked for too long – just like everything else.

The cooking times for meat will vary depending on how cold it is when you begin. It is best to remove it from the fridge some time before the cooking so that the meat has a chance to warm to room temperature. When it comes to be cooked there will be a much less steep temperature gradient between its inside and outside than if it had come straight from the fridge. When this does happen, the outside becomes cooked long before the inside is ready – just like hastily warmed frozen food. So for the best results you should remove joints of meat from the fridge at least three hours before you need it.

The other trick, and this applies to joints of meat especially, is to let them sit in the oven, after it has been turned off, for about a quarter of an hour. This allows the oven heat that is still in the meat to complete its cooking. If you serve the meat straight from the oven, you will find that it goes on cooking before your very eyes as you carve it, and it will lose a lot of its juices. The reason for the latter phenomenon is that, as the muscle fibres coagulate during the cooking, they exude moisture; think of twisting the strands of a wet rope or squeezing a wet towel. However, some of the protein coagulation is partially reversible, and the water-holding capacity of the tissues increases as the temperature drops. So by leaving the joint to sit for a little while, you are allowing it to cool down and revert to a state in which the joint will hold on to its liquid.

BEEF GOULASH

A spicy eastern European casserole of beef, peppers and soured cream. Boiled noodles or mashed potatoes go well with the beef. For greens, serve cabbage or beans, or follow with a crisp salad of endive or chicory.

Steps 1–9 may be carried out in advance.

Preparation time: 15–20 minutes
Cooking time: 2¼–2¾ hours

For Six Helpings:
2¾–3 lb/1.2–1.35 kg lean, good-quality stewing beef (cubed if possible in pieces the size of new potatoes)
2 medium-sized onions
2 cloves of garlic
2 tbs olive oil
1 heaped tbs plain flour
1 heaped tbs tomato paste
1½–2 tsp cayenne pepper
2 tsp salt (less if stock is very salty)
¾–1 pt/425–570 ml beef stock (use either home-made stock or make it up from stock cubes)
1 green pepper
1 red pepper
¼ pt/140 ml soured cream

1 Set the oven to Reg. 3 (325°F, 160°C).
2 If the meat has not been cut up by the butcher, dice it up into pieces, being careful to remove any gristle and fat first.
3 Peel and chop the onion and garlic finely.
4 Measure the olive oil into a large casserole, set it over a moderate heat and slide in the onion and garlic. Fry for a few minutes but don't let them brown.
5 Add the meat and brown the cubes all over. This should take about 5 minutes. Stir in the flour, cayenne pepper, salt and tomato paste.
6 Pour over sufficient stock to just cover the meat and, stirring all the time, bring the contents of the pot up to the boil.
7 Cover the casserole and transfer it to the oven for an hour's cooking.
8 Look at the stew to see how it's getting on, give it a stir and return it to the oven for another hour's cooking.
9 Take a piece of meat from the goulash to see if it is cooked. If it is, it should cut easily with a sharp knife and melt in your mouth. Turn off the oven and leave the casserole in it. If it's not ready, return the pot to the oven for another ½ hour and then repeat the test. The exact cooking time will depend on the size of the meat cubes and how cold the meat was when you began the preparations.
10 Remove the seeds from the peppers, chop into small pieces and add them to the stew.
11 Just before serving, stir in the soured cream (do not boil the goulash after the soured cream has been added, because it may curdle), taste and adjust the seasoning if necessary.

BEEF AND PORK STEW

The pork adds a succulent background to the beef but this is not a dish for slimmers. Serve the stew with boiled potatoes, or rice, and a green vegetable such as cabbage, broccoli, beans or peas. Red or white wine complements this hotpot.

Steps 1–11 may be carried out in advance.

Preparation time: 15–20 minutes
Cooking time: 2¼–2¾ hours

For Six Helpings:
- 1½ lb/680 g good-quality braising steak (if possible in chunks the size of new potatoes)
- 1 lb/455 g lean (shoulder) pork for braising (in pieces same size as beef)
- 1 large head fennel
- 3 carrots
- 1 large onion or 2 small ones
- 2–3 cloves garlic
- 2 tbs olive oil
- ¾ bottle (1 pt/570 ml) dry white wine
- 2 tsp salt
- pepper
- a few springs of parsley for garnishing

1 Heat the oven to Reg. 3 (325°F, 160°C).
2 Cut the meat into pieces if this has not yet been done.
3 Peel and chop the onion and garlic.
4 Remove the outer layer from the fennel head if it looks damaged and tough, and then wash and chop it roughly.
5 Peel, top and tail and slice the carrots into large pieces (1 inch/2 cm long).
6 Pour the olive oil into a casserole, add the onion and garlic and fry together gently, without browning, for a couple of minutes.

7 Add both the beef and the pork and fry for about 5 minutes until most of the meat is slightly browned.
8 Sprinkle over the salt and pepper, add the fennel and carrots and pour over the white wine.
9 Bring to the boil and then transfer the casserole to the oven for an hour.
10 Give the stew a stir and return it to the oven for another hour's cooking.
11 Remove a piece of meat and see whether it is cooked by cutting it with a sharp knife. It should flake apart easily and melt in your mouth. The exact time will depend on the thickness of the meat and how cold it was when the cooking began. If it is not ready, let the stew cook for another ½ hour.
12 Taste and adjust the seasoning if necessary and scatter the parsley over the stew.

ROAST SIRLOIN OF BEEF WITH YORKSHIRE PUDDING

Here is a recipe for a traditional English Sunday lunch. Serve the roast beef with the Yorkshire pudding cut into squares and gravy, roast or boiled potatoes and a green vegetable; mustard and horseradish sauce are the usual condiments. You may like a glass of red wine with the roast but many is the time I have been given sherry before Sunday lunch, and plenty of cider with the meal, by people who 'don't really drink' . . .

Preparation time: 20–25 minutes
Cooking time: 1¼ to just over 2 hours depending on how you like your beef: rare, medium-rare or well cooked.

For Six Helpings:
3½–4 lb/1.6–1.8 kg piece of boned and rolled sirloin
2 tsp salt
pepper

FOR THE YORKSHIRE PUDDING BATTER:
1 egg
4 oz/115 g plain flour
¼ pt/140 ml milk and ¼ pt/140 ml cold water mixed together
½ tsp salt
pepper
1–2 tbs dripping or oil

FOR THE GRAVY:
3 tbs beef fat from the cooking
1 tbs flour
¾ pt/425 ml stock or the same quantity of water vegetables have been cooked in plus ½ tsp marmite
¼ tsp salt
pepper

If you are preparing the batter with a machine, it won't need to sit after it has been made, so you can go straight to step 2 below; if not, you will need to mix it together and then let it stand for at least half an hour before the cooking, so follow these steps:

1a Sift the flour into a mixing bowl, add salt, some ground pepper and the egg.
1b Little by little start adding the liquid to the egg, as you do so drawing in the flour. Beat the mixture well to ensure it is smooth.
1c When about half the liquid has been incorporated pour in the remainder and beat the batter thoroughly until air bubbles break on the surface.
1d Cover the bowl and let it stand in a coolish place for at least half an hour.

2 About 15 minutes before you are going to put the beef in the oven, switch it to Reg. 6 (400°F/205°C). (Go to step 5 if 1 has been done.)
3 Sift the flour into the food-mixer, add the salt and drop in the egg.
4 Slowly start adding the milk and water mixture beginning with a thin trickle of liquid and making sure that you are producing a smooth batter. Continue with the liquid until it has all been added.
5 Rub the salt and pepper into the beef and put the joint in a roasting tin and slip it into the oven. Follow this regime for cooking the beef:

    rare: 15 minutes per lb or ½ kilo

    medium: 20 minutes per lb or ½ kilo

    well-done: 25 minutes per lb or ½ kilo.

At the end of the cooking lift the joint to a warmed plate and set in a warming-drawer, or cover it and leave it in a warm place, for 20–30 minutes. (Keep the juices for the gravy.)

6 About 10 minutes before the meat cooking ends, start the batter off.

7 Put the dripping or oil in another roasting tin and set it over moderate heat on the top of the stove. Pour in the batter and put the tin in the top of the oven and leave to cook for 30–35 minutes. The Yorkshire pudding should by then be ready; it will have puffed up and browned.

8 Once the meat has been removed from its roasting tin, you can prepare the gravy. Take 3 tbs beef juices for the gravy. If there is insufficient, make it up with a little melted butter; surplus juices can be poured over the beef.

9 Tilting the pan so that the juices are concentrated in one corner, stir in the flour. Slowly start adding the liquid so that you form a smooth sauce. Add the seasoning, taste and add more salt and pepper if necessary.

Variation

Yorkshiremen may tremble at the thought but a roughly chopped pepper and a tablespoon of sesame seeds scattered over the pudding before the cooking makes a deliciously unauthentic dish.

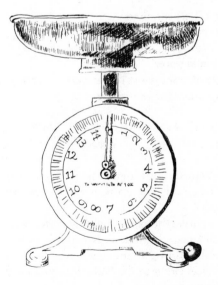

BEEF PIE

This is a rich pie of lean minced beef bound with an anchovy sauce, covered with pastry. Any of the cabbage family, beans, peas or carrots go well with it, and so does strong red wine.

Preparation time: 15–20 minutes
Cooking time: 60–70 minutes

For Six Helpings:
2–2½ lb/905–1,100 g lean minced beef
3–4 cloves garlic
1 tsp salt
pepper
nob of butter

FOR THE SAUCE:
2 oz/55 g butter
1½ oz/40 g flour
1 pt/570 ml milk
2 tbs anchovy purée

FOR THE PASTRY:
6 oz/170 g plain flour
3 oz/85 g butter
1 tsp salt
2 tbs cold water
optional: **few springs of watercress, parsley or**
coriander for garnishing

1 Set the oven to Reg. 5 (375°F, 190°C).
2 Grease a large ovenproof dish with the nob of butter.
3 Peel and chop the garlic finely and then mix it with the meat and a hearty grinding of pepper and the salt.
4 To make the sauce, melt the butter in a saucepan and then add the flour. Now slowly start adding the milk, stirring all the time so you form a lump-free sauce. Bring to the boil. (If it goes lumpy, put it through a sieve.)
5 Stir in the anchovy purée and then mix well with the meat and turn into the pie dish.
6 Prepare the pastry by cutting the butter into small pieces and adding it to the flour and salt. Then use your fingers to rub it into tiny pieces so that it mixes with the flour completely. You can check to see whether this has been achieved by shaking the bowl and observing whether any fat rises to the surface; if it does, rub it in.
7 Add the cold water and stir it in. Scatter some flour on a clean surface and on it roll out the pastry to a piece about one inch/2 cm larger than the top of the pie dish. Lay it over the meat, prick it in half a dozen places and then transfer it to the top of the oven for an hour.

ROAST CHICKEN WITH CURRY SAUCE

I have found this dish to be very popular on festive occasions. Boiled potatoes or rice and broccoli, beans or peas make nice accompaniments and so does red or white wine.

Preparation time: 10–15 minutes
Cooking time: 1–1¼ hours

For Four to Five Helpings:
1 fresh 3½ lb/1.6 kg chicken
½ oz/15 g butter
1 tbs olive oil
1–1½ tsp salt
pepper

FOR THE SAUCE:
2 tbs cooking juices
1 green pepper
½ tsp ground cumin
½ tsp ground coriander
1 tsp hot curry powder
1 dsp plain flour
2 tbs single cream
½ pt/285 ml stock (made from boiling the chicken giblets in ½ pt/285 ml water while the chicken cooks)

1 Set the oven to Reg. 5 (375°F, 190°C).
2 Unravel any string or rubber bands from the bird's body. Remove the liver, heart etc from the inside of the chicken; set the liver on one side and boil the rest with just over ½ pt/285 ml water to make stock; both will be used in the sauce.
3 Dribble the olive oil over a roasting tin.
4 Sprinkle the bird generously with salt (½ tsp or more) and pepper and lay it in the tin with the breasts facing down, i.e. 'upside down' (actually the right way up for the live bird); it will probably tilt over slightly to one side, leaving one leg and wing up in the air.
5 Take the butter and dot it in pieces over the exposed part of the bird.
6 Put the chicken in the oven and cook it for 25 minutes like this. Then tilt the other side upwards, sprinkle over a little more seasoning, baste with juices and cook for another 25 minutes.
7 Turn the chicken into its normal serving position and baste it with the juices; apply more salt and pepper and return it to the oven for a further 10–20 minutes.
8 Cut the liver into small pieces and dice the pepper finely.
9 At the end of the cooking time the chicken should be nicely browned, and the final sprinkling of salt will have made the skin crisp. Test to see if it is really cooked by plunging a knife into the flesh of an inner leg; it should draw no blood (it may look a little pink but don't worry because this is not due to raw muscle.) If it's not ready, let it cook for another 10 minutes and then test again.
10 Remove the bird to a serving dish, pour over some of the juices (keeping back 2 tbs for the sauce) and put it back in the turned-off oven.
11 Put the pepper and liver into the remaining juices and cook for a few minutes over a gentle heat.
12 Now add the spices and curry powder and then the flour, mix and cook for a minute. (It is best to tilt the pan so the mixture is concentrated in one corner.)
13 Start adding the stock (or water from cooked vegetables) slowly to the mixture, stirring all the time so you make a smooth sauce.
14 Lastly add the cream, taste and adjust the seasoning if necessary and bring the sauce to the boil.

POT-ROASTED WALNUT CHICKEN

This recipe uses walnuts in the stuffing; its richness is offset by lemon juice, which is added just before the bird is carved. Rice, potatoes or noodles and a green vegetable such as beans, cabbage or broccoli go well with this pot-roast. For wine, try something simple like Beaujolais or Rioja for red, or Muscadet if you prefer white wine.

Preparation time: 15–20 minutes
Cooking time: 1¼–1½ hours

For Five to Six Helpings:
1 fresh 3½ lb/1.6 kg chicken
1 tsp salt
pepper
1 oz/30 g butter
juice of 1 lemon
optional: **sprigs of parsley or watercress for garnishing**

FOR THE STUFFING:
1 thick slice of brown or white bread (to give
2 oz/55 g breadcrumbs)
½ onion
2 oz/55 g walnut pieces
1 oz/30 g butter
½ tsp salt
pepper

1 Set the oven to Reg. 4 (350°F, 175°C).
2 Remove any rubber bands or string from the bird, and the giblets from the inside of the chicken.
3 Now prepare the breadcrumbs for the stuffing. (Use a grater or an electric machine of some kind.)
4 Peel and chop the onion finely.

5 Melt the butter in a saucepan and to it add the onion. Let it cook gently for a couple of minutes but do not let it brown. Stir in the breadcrumbs, walnut pieces and seasoning and mix together well.
6 Fill the chicken with the stuffing and scatter over half the salt and some pepper.
7 Melt the other butter in a large casserole and to it add the stuffed chicken. Brown it all over and then set it so that the breasts face downwards; cover the pot and put it in the oven for an hour.
8 Turn the chicken so that it is the right way up for serving, shake over the rest of the salt and some more pepper and remove the lid from the pan.
9 Put the chicken back in the oven to cook for another 15 minutes. Test to see that it is cooked by inserting a sharp knife into the flesh of an inner leg. No blood should issue from the meat, even though it may look a little pink. If it is not ready, give it another 10 minutes cooking and then test once more.
10 Pour the lemon juice over the chicken and throw over the greenery if you so wish.

CHICKEN BREASTS WITH LEMON

The inspiration for this dish comes from Chinese cooking. The delicate combination of lemon, chicken and ginger with a little cream is very pleasing and it's just the right kind of thing to serve when you haven't got much time to spare. Boiled rice or potatoes and broccoli or beans go well with the chicken.

Steps 1–3 may be done in advance of the cooking.

Preparation time: 10–15 minutes
Cooking time: 20–25 minutes

For Six Helpings:
6 boneless breasts of chicken
1 tbs soy sauce
1 oz/30 g fresh ginger root
1 tbs olive/peanut oil

FOR THE SAUCE:
1½ lemons
water
1 heaped tsp cornflour
4 tbs single cream
pepper

1 Rub the soy sauce over the chicken breasts.
2 Grate the yellow part of the rind (avoiding the white pith) from the lemons. Squeeze the juice from the lemons and pour it into a measuring jug. Make it up to ⅔ pt/380 ml with water. Add the lemon peel.
3 Peel off the outer brown skin from the ginger and then grate it.
4 Heat the oil in a large frying-pan or wok and into it toss the ginger and chicken breasts. Fry these together for a minute or two and then add the lemon mixture and some pepper (the soy sauce provides the salt).
5 Bring to the boil, cover and leave to simmer very gently for 15–20 minutes, by which time the chicken should be firm but cooked.
6 Meanwhile mix the cornflour with 2 tbs water. When the chicken is cooked, add this and, stirring all the time, bring it back to the boil. (It will thicken as the cornflour cooks.) Simmer for one minute, add the cream, adjust the seasoning if necessary and serve.

CHICKEN LIVERS WITH DILL

Served with buttered toast or a mound of boiled rice, this dish is a meal on its own. If you wish to serve it as a first course, half these quantities should be ample for 6–8 helpings.

Preparation time: 10–15 minutes
Cooking time: about 15 minutes

For Four Helpings:
1½ lb/680 g chicken livers
1 onion
1½ oz/40 g butter
¼pt/140 ml water
2–3 tsp salt
freshly ground pepper
1 tbs dried dill weed or 3 tbs fresh dill

1 Pick over the livers, removing any white connective tissues.
2 Peel the onion and chop it finely.
3 Melt the butter in a pan and to it add the onion. Cook for a couple of minutes without letting it brown.
4 Add the chicken livers, seasoning and water. Cover the saucepan and let the livers simmer very gently for 10–15 minutes, giving them a stir twice.
5 Add the dill, taste and adjust the seasoning if necessary.

ROAST DUCK WITH VODKA AND GRAPEFRUIT JUICE

Preparation time: 5–10 minutes
Cooking time: 1½–1¾ hours

For Four Helpings:
1 duck weighing about 4 lb/1.8 kg
¼ pt/140 ml water
salt
pepper
1 tbs duck juices from cooking
juice of 1 grapefruit (¼ pt/140 ml)
1 tbs vodka

1 Heat the oven at Reg. 4 (350°F, 175°C) for 10 minutes.
2 Remove any giblets, liver and heart from the inside of the duck and put them, with the water, in a saucepan to simmer gently all the time the duck is cooking. Lay the duck upside down, on a wire rack, over a roasting tin (this will allow the fat to drip off as it cooks). Sprinkle over salt and pepper and then put it in the oven to cook, allowing 20 minutes per pound or half kilo.
3 When the bird is ready, transfer it to a serving dish and return it to the turned-off oven for 10 minutes.
4 Pour the surplus fat off the juices that have dripped from the duck, keeping only 1 tbs back, strain on the stock and add the vodka and grapefruit juice. Carve the duck and hand round the sauce separately.

ROAST LEG OF LAMB WITH GREEN PEPPERCORNS

I think the piquancy of the green peppercorns goes well with the slightly fatty nature of lamb. Serve the lamb with potatoes and green vegetables such as cabbage or courgettes. Beaujolais or claret is pleasing with the roast.

Preparation time: 10–15 minutes
Cooking time: 85–135 minutes

For Six Helpings:
Leg of lamb weighing 3½–4 lb/1.6–1.8 kg
2 tsp salt
pepper
optional: **2 cloves of garlic**

FOR THE SAUCE:
1 tbs green peppercorns (from a bottle of green peppercorns in brine)
½ small onion
2–3 tbs juices from the cooking
1 dsp flour
½ pt/285 ml water from cooked vegetables
2 tbs single cream
¼ tsp salt
pepper

1 Turn the oven on to Reg. 4 (350°F, 175°C).
2 Salt and pepper the meat and, if you like garlic, peel and slice it into thin slivers and press it into the flesh in a number of places.
3 Transfer the lamb to a roasting tin and put it in the oven. People vary in how they like lamb cooked so here are the approximate cooking times for rare, medium and well-cooked lamb:
　　rare (not as pink as rare beef): 20 minutes per lb or ½ kilo
　　medium: 25 minutes per lb or ½ kilo
　　well-cooked: 30 minutes per lb or ½ kilo
Baste the meat from time to time with the juices.
　　When the cooking time has elapsed, transfer the meat to its serving dish and put it back in the turned-off oven and leave it for another quarter of an hour.
4 To prepare the sauce, peel and chop the onion finely and chop up the green peppercorns. Add them to the meat juices in the pan. Cook together, over a gentle heat, for a couple of minutes.
5 Add the flour and stir it in well. Cook together for half a minute. You will find this, and the addition of the liquid, easier if you tilt the pan so that you concentrate the sauce base in one corner of the tin.
6 Add the water to the flour mixture SLOWLY, and blend it in carefully so that no lumps form.
7 Add the cream and seasoning and any juices that have accumulated around the sitting joint. Taste the sauce and adjust the seasoning if necessary.

BAKED LAMB CHOPS WITH POTATOES

Beer, cider or wine goes with this peasant-style casserole which can be prepared well before it is needed.

Preparation time: 20–25 minutes
Cooking time: about 1½ hours

For Six Helpings:
**6 chump lamb chops each weighing about 6–8 oz/
170–225 g or 8 smaller cutlets (each weighing
  about 4 oz/115 g)
3 lb/1.4 kg potatoes
2 tsp dried tarragon
3 leeks or 1 large onion
3 cloves of garlic
6 tbs olive oil
½ pt/285 ml dry white wine
3 tsp salt**

1 Set the oven to Reg. 5 (375°F, 190°C).
2 Begin by washing and peeling the potatoes. Then cut them into slices no thicker than a 50p coin.
3 Top and tail the leeks and remove their outer layers and slice into slivers, as you did for the potatoes. Wash them. If you are using an onion instead of the leeks, peel it and chop it up roughly.
4 Peel and chop the garlic finely.
5 Now dribble 2 tbs olive oil over the bottom and sides of a large casserole and use about a third of the potatoes to line the bottom of the pot. Add some salt and pepper.
6 Over the potatoes lay the meat with most of the fat left on (it makes it more succulent) and over it scatter the tarragon and a little more seasoning. Follow on with the garlic, then the sliced leeks (or onion) and finally pile on the rest of the sliced potatoes. Add salt and pepper once more.
7 Pour over the dry white wine and the remainder of the oil.
8 Put the full casserole over a moderate heat and bring it all up to the boil. Then cover it and transfer it to the oven for an hour.
9 Remove the lid and return the pot to the oven for another ½ hour's cooking. The potatoes should by then have browned nicely and the meat be tender.

POT ROAST OF SHOULDER OF LAMB

The cloves and cardamom give this dish an Eastern aroma.

Preparation time: 10–15 minutes
Cooking time: 1¾–2 hours

For Six Helpings:

3½–4 lb/1.6–1.8 kg boned and rolled piece of
    shoulder of lamb
1 oz/30 g butter
2 onions
¾ pt/425 ml water
2 cloves of garlic
5 cloves
3 green cardamom pods
2½ tsp salt
pepper
1½ oz/40 g breadcrumbs
¼ pt/140 ml single cream
3 egg yolks (juggle the yolks between the half shells
    as you drain off the whites)

1   Set the oven to Reg. 3 (325°F, 160°C).
2   Peel and chop the onion and garlic finely. Remove the cardamom from the pods and crush it.
3   Melt the butter in a large casserole and in it cook the onion and garlic for a few minutes, but do not let them brown.
4   Now brown the meat in the butter, pour on the water and add the seasoning, cardamom and cloves and bring to the boil.
5   Transfer the covered pot to the oven and leave it to cook for 1½–2 hours, depending on the size of the joint and how much you like lamb cooked.
6   Mix the cream with the egg yolks in a teacup.

7   Test to see whether the lamb is cooked: if a few red juices run out, it is ready, if you like lamb a little pink, but if you prefer it more cooked, return it to the oven for another half hour. When it is done to your taste, remove the joint to a serving dish and add the breadcrumbs, egg yolk and cream mixture to the cooking juices (do not bring to the boil because this will curdle the egg yolks). Taste the sauce, adjust the seasoning if necessary and hand it round with the carved meat.

SAUTÉED LAMBS' LIVER WITH MUSHROOMS

Here is a recipe for lambs' liver that takes only a few minutes to execute; it's most suitable for parties of four or less because the liver spoils if it is kept warm too long.

Preparation time: 5–10 minutes
Cooking time: 10–15 minutes

For Four Helpings:
1 lb/455 g lambs' liver sliced wafer thin – not more than ¼ inch/½ cm thick
8 oz/225 g mushrooms
1 small onion
2 oz/55 g butter
1 tsp French mustard
¼ pt/140 ml single cream
2 tsp salt
freshly ground black pepper

1   Peel the onion and dice it finely. Remove the stalks from the mushrooms (if you wish), peel them and then slice thinly.
2   Melt half the butter in a frying-pan and to it add the onion, mushrooms, 1 tsp salt and some pepper. Cover and cook for 5–10 minutes (until they are soft) and then remove them to a covered warm dish.
3   Mix the mustard with the cream in a teacup.
4   Now melt the rest of the butter in the pan and in it lay the liver, overlapping as little as possible, sprinkle over another teaspoon of salt and some pepper; cover the pan and let each side cook for 2–3 minutes over a moderate flame.
5   Stir in the mustard mixture and the mushrooms, taste and adjust the seasoning if necessary.

HAGGIS WITH MUSTARD SAUCE

This concoction of oatmeal and sheep viscera is traditionally served on 25 January, the anniversary of the birth of the Scottish poet Robert Burns.

I have noticed, in the last few years, that haggis can be bought in the shops most of the year, and as it is very good and inexpensive I serve it quite often with a mustard sauce and some cabbage or beans. Whisky is the customary tipple, but beer, cider or strong red wine does not harm the dish.

Preparation time: 10–15 minutes
Cooking time: 40–45 minutes

For Six Helpings:
2 haggis, each weighing 1–1½ lb/455–680 g

FOR THE SAUCE:
1½ oz/40 g butter
1 oz/30 g plain flour
¾ pt/425 ml milk
3 tbs single cream
1 heaped dsp French mustard
pepper
1 tsp salt

1   Set the oven to Reg. 4 (350°F, 175°C) and let it heat up for about 10 minutes.
2   Prick each haggis with a sharp knife in three or four places so that they won't burst as they cook.
3   Set them in an ovenproof dish and transfer them to the middle of the oven for 45 minutes cooking.
4   Now prepare the sauce. Melt the butter in a pan and then stir in the flour. Start adding the milk to the butter and flour mixture, slowly at first and then more rapidly as the sauce expands. Make sure it is always smooth and free of lumps. (If it does become lumpy, put it through a sieve.)
5   Bring the sauce up to the boil for a minute, to let

the flour cook, and then remove it from the heat and beat in the mustard, salt and pepper.

6 If you are going to use the sauce immediately, add all the cream but if you need to keep it hot for a while, keep back 1 tbs so that you can pour this over the surface of the sauce. This will help prevent a skin forming.

7 Remove the haggis from the oven when the cooking time is up and use a pair of scissors to open their casings. Scoop out the haggis onto individual plates and hand round the hot mustard sauce.

PIGEONS IN THE FIELD

Pigeons must be one of the cheapest forms of meat protein available *and* they taste good. Like all wild meat, the flesh is very lean, so lean that it can become dried out in the cooking. The way to get round this is to add some fat to lubricate the meat and keep it succulent. Boiled potatoes or noodles make good accompaniments.

Steps 1–8 may be carried out in advance.

Preparation time: 15–20 minutes
Cooking time: about 2 hours

For Six Helpings:
6 pigeons (in many shops and supermarkets they are sold 'oven ready')
1 large onion
4 cloves of garlic
4 tbs olive oil
8 oz/225 g streaky bacon
1 pt/570 ml beer (bitter)
3 tsp salt
ground black pepper

2½–3 lb/1.1–1.35 kg spinach
3 tsp salt
½ pt/285 ml water or less

1 Set the oven to Reg. 3 (325°F, 160°C).
2 Peel and chop the onion and garlic.
3 Remove the rind from the bacon and then cut it into pieces about 1 inch/2.5 cm long.
4 Look over the pigeons and see that they are ready to cook; remove any giblets from their insides if necessary.
5 Over the heat pour the olive oil into a large casserole and slide in the onion and garlic. Let them cook for a few minutes, but do not let them become brown.
6 Add the pigeons and brown all over. Then arrange the birds so that their breasts face down into the pan, with their flat surfaces uppermost. This should help the breast meat to remain moist.
7 Scatter over the bacon, salt and pepper and pour on the beer. Bring the brew to the boil, cover and transfer to the oven for 1½ hours.
8 Test to see whether they are cooked by inserting a sharp knife into a leg. It should go in and out easily. If they are not ready, give them another 20 minutes.
9 At least a quarter of an hour before you intend to serve the birds, prepare the spinach 'field'.
10 Heap the leaves into a sink of cold water and, removing the stalks, transfer them to a large pan. Add water and salt and boil the spinach for 5 minutes. Drain the cooked spinach very thoroughly.
11 Divide the spinach in six and make a green bed on each plate, and onto it rest a pigeon. Pour over some of the cooking juices.

ROAST PORK WITH CABBAGE

The spicy cabbage provides a pleasant foil to the rich pork meat. Serve the concoction with baked or boiled potatoes or rice. Strong red wine, such as Rioja, goes well with pork cooked in this fashion.

Preparation time: 10–15 minutes
Cooking time: about 2½ hours

For Six Helpings:
3½–4 lb/1.6–1.8 kg piece of boneless roasting pork
   (loin, shoulder or leg)
1 tsp salt
pepper

A green cabbage such as January King weighing
   about 2½–3 lb/1.1–1.35 kg
1½ tsp salt
3 pt/1.7 l water

3 fresh green chillis
3–4 cloves of garlic
2 tbs pork juices
pepper
salt to taste

1 Heat the oven at Reg. 4 (350°F, 175°C) for 10 minutes or so.
2 Scatter the salt and pepper over the joint, put it in a roasting tin and then transfer it to the oven. Leave the pork to cook, allowing 40 minutes for each pound (half kilo) of flesh. Pork should always be well cooked, so be sure that no red juices whatsoever come from the joint when you come to test it. Do by all means look at it from time to time but please don't ever baste the skin with the cooking juices. If you do this, you will turn it from delicious crackling to tough leather.

3 When the pork is cooked, put it on a serving dish and put it back in the turned-off oven. Retain a couple of tablespoonfuls of the juices for frying the spices.
4 Now put the cabbage water (salted) on to boil in a large pot.
5 Remove the outer leaves of the cabbage, quartering and coring it and slicing it up. Wash it and then add to the boiling water. Cook for 4–5 minutes.
6 While the cabbage is cooking, remove the seeds from the chillis under cold water (so that their vapours are washed away rather than going up to your eyes) and chop them up very finely.
7 Peel and chop the garlic finely.
8 Into the fat throw the garlic and chillis. Cook together for a few minutes.
9 Drain the water from the cabbage and arrange it around the pork, and heap the spicy mixture over the cabbage.

PORK CASSEROLE WITH BEANS

A substantial dish for a cold January evening. The beans, because they are cooked with the pork, acquire a delicious flavour; any kind of vegetable goes well with it. Potato buffs will probably insist on their customary dose too, though I think the beans are sufficient.

The casserole can easily be cooked the day before it is to be eaten. It will take a good half hour to re-heat properly.

Preparation time: 15–20 minutes, plus one hour for the bean soaking time
Cooking time: about 2½ hours

For Six Helpings:
1 lb/455 g dried haricot beans
2 pt/1.1 l meat stock (made from cubes or even better from bones)
3½–4 lb/1.6–1.8 kg boneless piece of pork (leg, loin, or shoulder)
1 tbs olive oil or meat fat
2 carrots
1 onion
3 cloves of garlic
2 sticks of celery
few sprigs of fresh herbs or 1 dsp mixed dried herbs
1 dsp salt
pepper

1 Follow this quick method for soaking the beans. Bring the stock to the boil, add the dried beans, return to the boil and simmer for 1–2 minutes. Let the beans stand in the stock for an hour.
2 Meanwhile set the oven to Reg. 3 (325°F, 160°C) and start preparing the rest of the casserole ingredients.
3 Peel the carrots and chop them up roughly. Peel the onion and garlic and dice them finely. Wash the celery and chop it up roughly.
4 Melt the fat in a big casserole and into it throw all the vegetables. Let them cook for a minute or two but do not let them brown.
5 Add the joint of pork and brown it all over. Add salt and pepper and herbs and transfer the casserole to the oven for 1½ hours.
6 Bring the beans back to the boil and add them, and their liquid, to the pork and return to the oven for another hour's cooking. Pork needs 40 minutes per pound or half kilo, so you can calculate the exact cooking time. It should always be well cooked, so be sure that no pink juices whatsoever come out of it when you stick a knife in the flesh to test it. Then taste and adjust the seasoning if necessary.

VARIATIONS
Sausages (allow 2 lb/905 g for six helpings) can be substituted for the joint of pork. The beans should be added with them, and the cooking takes about one hour. A tablespoon of tomato paste also makes a nice addition.

Lamb is good cooked in this fashion too. For six helpings you will need a boneless piece of lamb shoulder (or other stewing cut) weighing approximately 3½ lb/1.6 kg. Follow the above recipe but add the beans only half an hour after the meat cooking has been initiated in step 5, not one hour. The casserole will take 1½–2 hours to cook, depending on how you like lamb.

PORK FILLET WITH WATERCRESS SAUCE

The piquant watercress sauce goes well with pork.

Preparation time: 10–15 minutes
Cooking time: 20–25 minutes

For Six Helpings:
6 pork escalopes (fillet beaten thin) each weighing about 4–6 oz/115–170 g
1 oz butter
1 tbs olive oil
2–3 tsp salt
pepper

FOR THE SAUCE:
2 bunches (about 8 oz/225 g) watercress
1 ½ oz/40 g butter
1 oz/30 g plain flour
3/4 pt/425 ml milk
1 tsp salt
pepper

1. Melt the butter with the olive oil in a large frying-pan and then add the pork. Scatter over half the seasoning, cover the pan and leave to cook for 15–20 minutes, turning them over after about 10 minutes and adding the rest of the seasoning.
2. Meanwhile begin to prepare the sauce by removing the stalks from the watercress.
3. Melt the butter in a pan and stir in the flour. Start adding the milk to the roux (butter and flour mixture), slowly at first and then more rapidly as the sauce increases in volume. Try to ensure it is smooth, but any lumps will be removed in the next step.
4. Stir in the salt, pepper and watercress and then purée the sauce in a liquidizer or food processor.
5. Return the sauce to the pan and adjust the seasoning if necessary. Pour some sauce over each escalope and serve.

BOILED GAMMON WITH PARSLEY SAUCE

Like so much of English food, gammon is quite under-rated; it is delicious and relatively inexpensive. I think potatoes and leeks, or carrots, go well with this dish.

Preparation time: 10–15 minutes
Cooking time: about 75 minutes

For Six Helpings:
3 lb/1.35 kg piece of boiling gammon (suitable cuts are slipper, prime collar, hock or corner)
2–2½ pt/1.1–1.4 l water or sufficient to almost cover the gammon
pepper

FOR THE SAUCE:
1 oz/30 g butter
1 oz/30 g flour
½ onion
¾ pt or/425 ml milk
2 oz/55 g parsley
1 tsp salt
pepper
¼ pt/140 ml cream

1 Put the gammon in a casserole or large saucepan and pour over the water. Add some pepper, but no salt because the gammon will have quite a bit in it.
2 Set the gammon over the heat and when it reaches boiling adjust the heat so it simmers gently for one hour. It will need to simmer for 25 minutes for each pound or half kilo of meat.
3 After about three-quarters of an hour start to prepare the sauce by removing the parsley leaves from the stalks and chopping them up very finely. Discard the tough stalks.
4 Peel and chop the onion.
5 Melt the butter in a saucepan and then add the chopped onion. Allow it to cook for several minutes but on no account let it brown.
6 Now stir in the flour.
7 Start to add the milk very slowly to the roux (butter and flour mixture) and beat it in to form a smooth thick paste. Continue adding the milk slowly being careful to mix it in thoroughly before adding some more; as you go on the mixture will be easier to manage.
8 Add salt, pepper and the parsley.
9 If you are going to serve the sauce immediately stir in all the cream, taste it and adjust the seasoning if necessary. If you need to keep it hot for a little while use half the mixture to coat the top of the sauce (to prevent a skin forming) and then, when you reheat it, add the remainder of the cream.
10 Remove the gammon from the water*, carve and serve with the sauce.

* Do not throw away the water; it will make excellent stock for a soup or casserole.

HAM AND BEAN SPROUTS

Here is a quick stir-fry recipe that calls for using a wok, if possible.

Preparation time: 10–15 minutes
Cooking time: 8–10 minutes

For Six Helpings:
1¼ lb/570 g thickly sliced cooked ham
1 lb/455 g bean sprouts
1½ lb/680 g raw chicory or cooked vegetables such
   as beans, peas, celery, potato
2 oz/55 g ginger root
3 cloves garlic
2 tbs peanut/olive oil
1 tbs soy sauce
2 tbs sesame oil
1–2 tsp salt
pepper

1   Chop the meat into pieces the size of 50p coins.
2   Remove the outer leaves from the chicory and chop roughly.
3   Peel and grate the ginger. Peel and chop the garlic finely.
4   Fry the ginger and garlic in the peanut oil for a couple of minutes, without letting them brown.
5   Add the meat, bean sprouts, chicory, sesame oil, soy sauce and seasoning and mix together well. Cover the pan and let the mixture fry for 5–8 minutes, with the occasional stir. Taste and adjust the seasoning if necessary.

VARIATIONS

Any other cooked meat, or prawns, can be used instead of the ham.

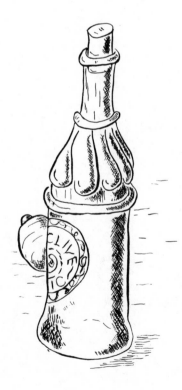

Pasta and rice

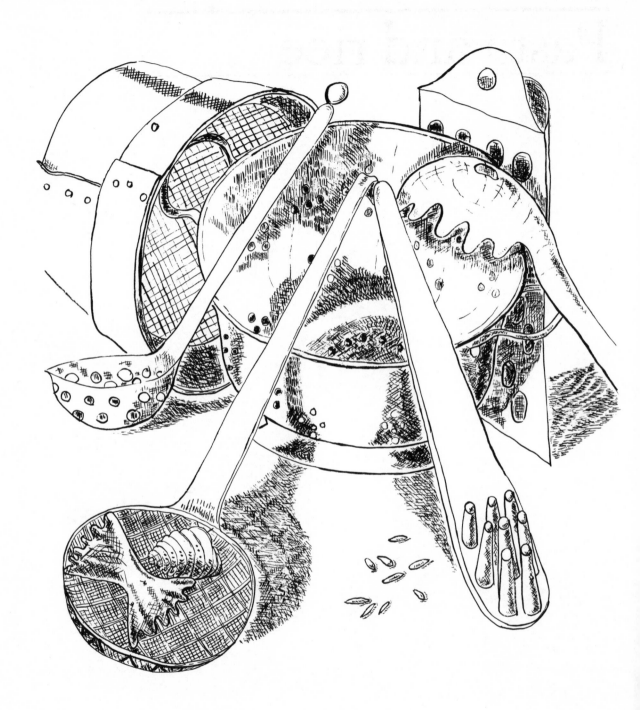

Pasta and rice

First, some general guidelines on cooking pasta and rice. As a rule you need to allow 2–3 oz/55–85 g of dried pasta per helping and about ¾–1 pt/425–570 ml water and ½ tsp salt. Add the pasta to the boiling water and simmer for 8–12 minutes depending on the type. Drain and add butter and pepper. (See pasta packets for instructions too.) Fresh pasta needs to be cooked for only 2–3 minutes, and 4–6 oz/115–170 g cooked in ½–¾ pt/285–425 ml will satisfy most appetites.

The quantities are the same for white rice, but the cooking is slightly different. If you like the grains of cooked rice to be separate, wash it first and then boil it in salted water, allowing ½ tsp salt and ½–¾ pt/285–425 ml water per helping as before. Stir to prevent it 'catching' on the bottom of the pan and leave it to simmer, with the lid on the pan, for 12–15 minutes. It will have increased in volume substantially. The rice is cooked when it has lost its crunchiness. Drain the rice through a sieve and add butter and pepper. In the alternative method all the water is absorbed during the cooking, and the cooked rice sticks together in a mass. So for a 2–3 oz/55–85 g helping boil it in twice its volume of water – that is, about 3½–5 fl oz/100–150 ml for 12–15 minutes, giving it a stir from time to time.

Brown rice takes longer to cook: 25–50 minutes depending on the variety (see the packet instructions) but the quantities per helping are the same as white rice. A good way to keep rice warm is to turn it into a sieve which you set over a little simmering water and cover. It can be inverted onto a plate to form a dome to serve.

In the following recipes the quantities of pasta and rice per helping are greater because they are intended to be the backbone of a meal.

PASTA WITH FISH AND BASIL

Preparation time: 5–10 minutes
Cooking time: 12–15 minutes

For Six Helpings:
1 lb/455 g dried pasta (tagliatelle, shells, quills)
3 tsp salt
4½ pt/2.5 l water
1 oz/30 g butter

FOR THE SAUCE:
1 onion
1½ lb/680 g shelled mussels, prawns, cockles or
other cooked, boned fish such as salmon, tuna or
haddock
4 oz/115 g pesto sauce (sold in jars in many
delicatessens)
1 oz/30 g butter
pepper

1 Boil the pasta in the salted water for 10–12 minutes or until just cooked. Drain and stir in the butter.
2 Peel and chop the onion finely and fry in a very large pot or wok in the butter for 5–10 minutes until soft, without letting it become brown.
3 Add the fish and then stir in the pesto sauce. Taste and adjust the seasoning if necessary and mix with the pasta.

VARIATION

A green or red pepper, roughly diced, may be added at step 2 if you like it soft or at step 3 if you prefer it crunchy. A few left-over vegetables would not go amiss in the sauce either.

SPAGHETTI BOLOGNESE

I hope this recipe helps, just a little, to put the record straight about bolognese sauce: it can be absolutely delicious. Remember to have plenty of Parmesan cheese to hand; it is best to buy a slab (it keeps well) and then grate it yourself.

For wine, choose some strong red Italian, Spanish or Bulgarian.

Preparation time: 15–20 minutes
Cooking time: 30 minutes

For Six Helpings:
18 oz/510 g dried spaghetti
6 pt/3.4 l water
1 tbs salt
1 oz/30 g butter
(For big eaters allow 24 oz/680 g spaghetti and
8 pt/4.5l water)

FOR THE SAUCE:
1 lb/455 g lean minced beef
4 oz/115 g unsmoked bacon
4 oz/115 g chicken livers
1 tbs olive oil
1 onion
2 cloves garlic
2 tbs porridge oats
2 tbs tomato paste
1 heaped tsp mixed dried herbs
½ pt/285 ml meat stock or water
¼ pt/140 ml dry white wine
¼ pt/140 ml single cream
1½ tsp salt
pepper

1 Peel and chop the onion into small pieces. Peel and chop the garlic finely.

2 Remove the rind from the bacon and cut it and the chicken livers into crouton-size pieces.

3 Over a moderate heat pour the oil into a large saucepan or casserole. Add the chopped onion and garlic and fry together for a minute, but do not let them become brown.

4 Now add the minced beef and fry for a few minutes to brown it.

5 Add the bacon and livers and sprinkle on the porrridge oats (they will thicken the sauce). Stir and fry the mixture for a minute.

6 Add the tomato paste, herbs, salt and pepper and then the stock or water and wine.

7 Stirring from time to time, bring to the boil and then adjust the heat so that the mixture simmers gently, with the lid on the pan, for half an hour. Look at it occasionally to make sure it isn't 'catching' on the bottom of the pot, and give the mixture a turn.

8 The spaghetti will take 10–12 minutes to cook, so after the sauce has been boiling for about 20 minutes begin cooking the pasta. Fill another saucepan with the water, add salt, bring to the boil and add the spaghetti and let it simmer for about 10 minutes, when it should be tender but not too soft. Test it to see if it's ready.

9 Drain off the water and add the butter and shake the pan so that it coats all the spaghetti. Cover and keep warm.

10 Add the cream to the bolognese, taste and adjust the seasoning if necessary. Bring the sauce back to the boil briefly.

PASTA WITH CHILLIS AND SAUSAGE

Here is a dish that combines ingredients from the Orient and Europe. Drink beer, lager or water with it; wine will be lost in the fiery flavours.

Preparation time: 10–15 minutes
Cooking time: 15–20 minutes

For Six Helpings:
14 oz/396 g dried pasta (bows, shells, quills, gnocchi)
4 pt/2.3 l water
2 tsp salt
1½ lb/680 g spicy smoked sausage such as chorizos, salami or black pudding or a mixture
4 fresh green chillis
4 cloves of garlic
2 tbs olive or peanut oil
1 tsp salt

1 Set the salted water on to boil and when it is ready throw in the pasta and simmer for 12–15 minutes.

2 Meanwhile remove the tops and seeds from the chillis under running water and then chop them very finely. Wash your hands thoroughly afterwards, to rinse off any chilli.

3 Peel and chop the garlic finely. Slice the sausage into discs about ¼ inch/0.5 cm thick.

4 Five minutes before the pasta cooking time is up, heat the oil in a large frying-pan or wok and in it fry the chillis and garlic for a minute or two, but do not let them become brown.

5 Add the sliced sausage and salt and let the ingredients fry together gently until the pasta is ready.

6 Test to see that the pasta is cooked, drain off the water and then add it to the fry-up. Toss everything together.

TAGLIATELLE WITH MUSHROOMS

Serve this dish with plenty of freshly grated Parmesan cheese (about 2 oz/55 g should be sufficient). It is very simple to prepare, and steps 1–3 may be carried out in advance. To make it a first course, halve the quantities.

Preparation time: 5–10 minutes
Cooking time: 10–15 minutes

For Six Helpings:
1½ lb/680 g dried tagliatelle (green or white)
water
salt
2 oz/55 g butter

FOR THE SAUCE:
2½ lb/1.1 kg flat mushrooms
2 onions
3 oz/85 g butter
3 tbs dry sherry
1 dsp dried chervil
3 tsp salt
pepper

1 Peel and chop the onions finely. Peel the mushrooms, remove their stalks (if you wish) and then slice them into nuggets.
2 Melt the butter in a pan and to it add the onion. Cook for a few minutes, but do not let it brown.
3 Add the mushrooms, chervil, sherry and seasoning and then let the sauce simmer gently, with the pan covered, for about 10 minutes.
4 Meanwhile boil the salted water, add the pasta and let it simmer for 8 minutes.
5 Drain the water from the tagliatelle and then coat it with butter and serve with the sauce.

PORK FILLET BAKED WITH RICE

It was a wonderful moment when I discovered that white rice cooked in exactly the same time as pork fillet. I think it is best to serve a vegetable, or salad, after this fairly substantial dish, and wash it down with some potent wine or beer.

Preparation time: 10–15 minutes
Cooking time: 30–35 minutes

For Seven to Eight Helpings:
1¾–2 lb/795–905 g pork fillet
2 onions
4 cloves of garlic
8 dried juniper berries
2 tbs olive oil
1 lb/455 g white rice
2 pt/1.1 1 meat stock – either fresh stock or made from cubes
1–1½ level tsp salt (depends how salty is the stock)
freshly ground pepper
optional: a few sprigs of parsley or watercress for garnishing

1 Set the oven to Reg. 4 (350°F, 175°C).
2 Remove any white stringy matter and fat from the fillets and then slice them into medallions a little thicker than 50p pieces.
3 Peel and chop the onion and garlic. Crush the juniper berries.
4 Pour the oil into a large casserole and in it fry the onion and garlic for a couple of minutes.
5 Add the pork and rice and fry for a further couple of minutes, stirring all the time.
6 Pour in the stock, add the berries and seasoning and bring to the boil.

7 Transfer the casserole to the oven and leave to cook for 25–30 minutes. By this time the rice should be ready and have absorbed most of the liquid, and the pork should be tender. Garnish with greenery, if you have it.

MIXED FRIED RICE

Like all Oriental dishes, this requires very little cooking but a fair amount of preparation if you are beginning with raw ingredients. On the other hand it's a very useful way to use up left-over cooked vegetables or rice. You will need a wok or a large deep frying-pan for the best results.

Preparation time: 10–15 minutes
Cooking time: 10 minutes

For Four Helpings:
2½ lb/1.1 kg cooked white rice (13 oz/370 g cooked in 2 pt/1.1 l water will give this quantity. It needs to be cooked so that the grains remain separate.)
1 lb/455 g cooked vegetables – a mixture of say 3 or 4 of the following would be best: green or white cabbage, carrots, mange-touts, leeks, broccoli, peas, beans, mushrooms
3–4 fresh green chillis
4 cloves of garlic
2 oz/55 g fresh ginger root
4 tbs peanut oil
2–3 tsp salt
freshly ground pepper

1 Remove the seeds from the chillis under running water and then chop them into tiny pieces.
2 Peel and grate the ginger. Peel and chop the garlic finely.
3 Go through the cooked vegetables and see that they are all about the same size and can easily be eaten with a fork (or chopsticks).
4 Pour the oil into a wok or frying-pan, set it over moderate heat and to it add the chillis, ginger and garlic. Fry together for a couple of minutes.
5 Now add the rice, vegetables and seasoning and continue frying for another 5–8 minutes over a brisk heat, turning it regularly so that it browns and some of the rice becomes crisp.

KEDGEREE

Indian in origin, it once graced Victorian breakfast sideboards but now it is served more often as a simple lunch or supper dish. It is very good and a meal in itself, though it could be followed by a salad. Beer or wine drinks well with it.

Preparation time: 10–15 minutes
Cooking time: 20–25 minutes

For Six Helpings:
1 lb/455 g raw rice
2 pt/1.1 l water (or 3 lb cooked white rice)
1 dsp salt

2 lb/905 g fillets of smoked haddock (skinned if possible)
3 eggs
2 tbs olive oil
1 onion
1 dsp garam masala
2 peppers (green, red or yellow)
pepper

1 Put the eggs in a small saucepan, cover with water, gradually bring them to boiling point and let them simmer for 10 minutes. At the end of this time pour off the hot water and immediately immerse them in cold water to cool them down quickly and prevent that nasty grey line appearing between the yolk and the white. (This is due to the formation of particles of iron sulphide on the surface of the yolk.) When you can handle them, peel and slice them roughly.

2 If you have been unable to purchase skinned fish, you will need to remove the skin. Hold the fillets flat on a surface, skin side down, with one hand and with the other use a knife to separate the flesh from the skin. Cut through the flesh down to the skin and then ease the flesh away as you draw the knife under it. It helps if you go with the grain of the fish. Cut into pieces the size of new potatoes.

3 Peel and chop the onion finely. Remove the seeds from the peppers and chop them up roughly.

4 Pour the oil into a large pan and fry the onion, without letting it brown, for a few minutes.

5 Stir in the rice and fry for another minute or two and then add the water, salt and pepper. Cover the pan and simmer for 8 minutes.

6 Stir in the fish, peppers, eggs and spice and simmer for another 5 minutes.

7 Taste and adjust the seasoning if necessary.

Vegetarian dishes

Vegetarian dishes

You do not have to be a vegetarian to enjoy vegetarian dishes: I, for one, generally have at least one vegetarian meal a day, and could not wish otherwise. I suppose one of the reasons, economy aside, is that they give gastronomic satisfaction without that 'heavy' feeling meat dishes so often leave in one's body.

There is an enormous variety of tempting raw ingredients with which to experiment; here are a few offerings of recipes using an assortment of Eastern and Western foods.

BAKED POTATOES INDONESIAN STYLE

The spicy sauce that accompanies the potatoes is pretty rich, so a little goes a long way. My sister says that any cold left-over sauce makes delicious sandwich filling.

Preparation time: 10–15 minutes
Cooking time: 45–60 minutes

For Six Helpings:
6 large potatoes for baking

FOR THE SAUCE:
2 spring onions or ½ small onion
2 cloves of garlic
1 oz/30 g fresh ginger root
3–4 fresh green chillis
1 dsp peanut/olive oil
½ jar (i.e. 6 oz/170 g) crunchy peanut butter
½ pt/285 ml coconut milk (made from 2 oz/55 g of dried coconut powder or 4 oz/115 g creamed coconut and ½ pt/285 ml hot water)
1 lemon
2 tsp soy sauce
1 tsp salt
pepper

1 Heat the oven at Reg. 5 (375°F, 190°C) for ten minutes.
2 Wash the potatoes and remove any blemishes from their skins. Prick them in a couple of places and then put them in the oven for about 45 minutes.
3 Peel and finely chop the spring onion and garlic. Peel the ginger and grate it. Cut the chillis in half and remove the seeds (do this under running water) and chop them up very finely too.
4 Squeeze the juice from the lemon.
5 Put the spring onion, garlic, ginger and chillis in a saucepan and fry together gently in the oil for about five minutes.
6 Add the peanut butter and then stir in the coconut milk, lemon juice, soy sauce, salt and pepper. Let the brew simmer for five minutes.
7 Taste and adjust the seasoning if necessary. Add a little water to the sauce if you think it is too thick.
8 Check the potatoes when their time is up by inserting a sharp knife into them; if it goes in easily, they are ready. Cut the potatoes in half and heap sauce over each half.

CABBAGE WITH NUTS

This dish is good served with Genoan potatoes (p. 101).

Preparation time: 10–15 minutes
Cooking time: 10–15 minutes

For Six Helpings:
2 Savoy cabbages (or another kind of green cabbage to yield 2 lb oz/905 g cabbage leaves)
2 oz/55 g butter
2 tbs peanut/olive oil
8 oz/225 g chopped nuts and seeds (for example brazils, almonds, walnuts, peanuts, pecans, cashews, sesame, sunflower seeds or pine kernels)
4 oz/115 g breadcrumbs
2–3 tsp salt
pepper

1 Chop the cabbage and wash it.
2 Melt the butter with the oil in a large pan (a wok preferably) and to it add the cabbage, nuts, breadcrumbs and seasoning. Fry, stirring the mixture from time to time, with the pan covered for 10–15 minutes until the cabbage has just lost its crunch and the nuts and crumbs are browned.
3 Taste and adjust the seasoning if necessary.

BRUSSELS SPROUTS IN CELERY SAUCE

Serve this hot winter supper dish with baked potatoes.

Preparation time: 10–15 minutes
Cooking time: 25–30 minutes

For Four to Five Helpings:
2 lb/905 g Brussels sprouts
1 pt/570 ml water
2 tsp salt

FOR THE SAUCE:
2 heads of celery
1 clove of garlic
2 tsp salt
2 oz/55 g butter
2 oz/55 g flour
1 pt/570 ml milk
pepper

1 oz/30 g poppy seeds
1 oz/30 g sesame seeds

1 First prepare the celery for the sauce. Discard the outer stalks and then top and tail the rest, wash and slice into pieces about ½ inch/1 cm long.
2 Peel and chop the garlic finely.
3 Melt the butter in a pan and add the chopped celery, garlic and salt. The salt will make the celery exude a little water so there is no need to add any.
4 Cover the pan and let the celery cook for 15–20 minutes until it is just tender. Look at it from time to time to see the butter isn't browning.
5 While the celery is cooking, prepare the sprouts in the usual way by removing the outer leaves and stalk and making a cross with a knife in the base. Wash them.
6 Set the salted water for the sprouts on to boil.
7 By now the celery should be tender and soft and you can make the sauce. Add the flour and stir it in well.
8 Start adding the milk, slowly at first and then more rapidly as you go on, making sure that you always end up with an absolutely smooth, lump-free mixture. Add pepper and more salt if necessary. Keep it warm while you cook the sprouts.
9 Cook the sprouts in the boiling water for 5–8 minutes. Turn the grill on high.
10 Drain off the cooking water, turn the sprouts into a serving dish and over them pour the hot sauce.
11 Sprinkle over the poppy and sesame seeds and brown under the grill for 5–10 minutes.

CASSEROLE OF MIXED VEGETABLES

This is nice served with a dusting of sesame seeds or the parsley sauce on p. 70.

Preparation time: 10–15 minutes
Cooking time: 45–55 minutes

For Six Helpings:
2 lb/905 g potatoes
1 lb/455 g carrots
2 onions/3 leeks
1 head celery/2 heads fennel
1½ oz/40 g butter
¼ pt/140 ml water
2–3 tsp salt
pepper

1   Set the oven to Reg. 4 (350°F, 175°C).
2   Peel the potatoes and carrots and chop them roughly. Peel and slice the onions or leeks. Wash the celery, or fennel, removing any tough outer stems and then chop roughly.
3   Melt the butter in a large pot and into it throw all the vegetables and fry gently for 5 minutes.
4   Pour on the water, add the seasoning and bring to the boil. Cover the casserole and transfer it to the oven for 40–50 minutes.

SPICY BEAN HOTPOT

This isn't a grand dish by any means but it's very satisfying, and the chillis make it rather unusual – and lively.

Preparation time: 20–25 minutes plus one hour for the beans to soak
Cooking time: 40–50 minutes

For Six Helpings:
1½ lb/680 g dried butter beans
4 pt/2.3 l water
1 tbs salt

FOR THE SAUCE:
4 tbs olive or peanut oil
4 cloves garlic
3–4 fresh green chillis
1 lb/455 g mushrooms
4 tbs tomato paste
½ pt/285 ml water
2 tsp salt
pepper
12 oz/340 g mild goats' cheese, Brie or other soft
   creamy cheese
optional: a few sprigs of parsley for garnishing

1   Follow this quick method for soaking dried beans. Bring the water to the boil in a large pot, add the dried beans, return to the boil and simmer for 2 minutes. Then remove the beans from the heat and let them stand in the hot water for one hour.
2   Bring the bean and water mixture to the boil once more, add the salt, and let them simmer for 30–40 minutes, when the beans should be tender. Stir them from time to time to prevent their catching on the bottom of the pan.
3   While the beans are cooking, prepare the ingredients for the sauce. Remove the stems from the mushrooms, peel them and then slice into pieces about ¼ inch/0.5 cm thick.
4   Peel the garlic cloves and chop them finely. Remove the seeds from the chillis under running water and then chop them up finely like the garlic.
5   Cut the rind from the cheese and dice it into nuggets.
6   Using either a wok or a saucepan, heat the olive oil and into it toss the garlic, chillis, mushrooms, salt and pepper. Cover the pan and let the contents sauté gently for 5 minutes over a moderate heat.
7   Stir in the tomato paste and water. Drain the water from the beans and add them. Let the concoction simmer gently for a couple of minutes. Just before serving, stir in the cheese (and scatter over the parsley).

GRATIN OF CAULIFLOWER, OLIVES AND FENNEL

Serve the gratin by itself or with thick slices of bread and butter.

Steps 1–10 may be done in advance of the final cooking.

Preparation time: 15–20 minutes
Cooking time: 25–35 minutes

For Six Helpings:
2 medium-size cauliflowers
1 large head of fennel
2 pt/1.1 l water
2 tsp salt
3 oz/85 g stoned green or black olives
nob of butter

FOR THE SAUCE:
3–4 cloves of garlic
4 oz/115 g butter
3 oz/85 g flour
1¾ pt/995 ml milk
2 heaped dsp tomato paste
2 tsp salt
pepper
¼ pt/140 ml single cream
4 oz/115 g Parmesan or other strong hard cheese

1　Set the oven to Reg. 6 (400°F, 205°C). Grease a large ovenproof dish with the nob of butter.
2　First prepare the sauce. Grate the cheese; peel the garlic and chop it up finely.
3　Melt the butter in a pan and when it starts to foam add the garlic. Cook for a minute and then stir in the flour and cook together for another minute.
4　SLOWLY start to add the milk to the roux (butter and flour mixture). In between each addition beat well so that you form a smooth paste. As the sauce increases in volume and becomes thinner, you may add the liquid more rapidly but always ensure you have mixed in one lot before adding any more. (If it is lumpy, put it through a sieve.)
5　Stir in the tomato paste, salt and pepper and bring the sauce up to boiling point. Stir in half the grated cheese and dribble the cream over the sauce but do not stir it in until just before pouring it over the vegetables in step 10 (the cream coating will help prevent a skin forming).
6　Set the water on to boil, with the salt, for the vegetables.
7　Cut the cauliflowers up into florets, discarding the central thick stalk but retaining a few leaves if you like them. Wash the fennel, quarter it, remove the core and slice it roughly.
8　Cook the vegetables in the boiling water for 3–4 minutes; the cauliflower should still be a little crisp.
9　Drain the water from the cooked vegetables and turn them into the dish. Sprinkle over the olives.
10　Now smother the vegetables with the red sauce and finish off with the rest of the grated cheese.
11　Slip the dish into the top part of the hot oven and leave it to cook for 15–20 minutes. It is ready when the sauce is bubbling and the cheese is brown.

GRATIN OF VEGETABLES

This cheese sauce can be poured over almost any vegetable, or mixture, to make a very satisfying dish.

Preparation time: 10–15 minutes
Cooking time: 20–25 minutes

For Six Helpings:
2½ lb/1.1 kg prepared vegetables (for example, carrots, beans, cauliflower, courgettes, potatoes)
water for cooking vegetables
2–3 tsp salt
nob of butter

FOR THE SAUCE:
3½ oz/100 g butter
3 oz/85 g flour
1¾ pt/995 ml milk
2 tsp salt
pepper
¼ pt/140 ml single cream
4 oz/115 g Cheddar cheese
4 oz/115 g Gruyère or Emmenthal cheese

1 Turn the oven to Reg. 6 (400°F, 205°C). Grease a large open dish.
2 While the vegetables are cooking (see table pp. 96–8) in the salted water, prepare the sauce. First grate the cheeses, keeping them separate.
3 Melt the butter in a pan and to it add the flour. Start to add the milk to the butter and flour roux, very slowly at first so you form a smooth paste and then a sauce. (If it becomes lumpy, put it through a sieve.)
4 Stir in the salt, pepper, Cheddar cheese and cream. Taste and adjust the seasoning if necessary.
5 Drain the water from the vegetables and put them in the dish. Pour over the sauce, scatter on the Gruyère or Emmenthal and cook in the oven for 15–20 minutes, when the top should be bubbling and nicely browned.

WATERCRESS OMELETTE

Here is a very simple, but rather unusual, supper dish. Serve the omelette (hot or cold) with bread and a green salad. It also makes a stylish first course for a grander meal; if you do this, halve the quantities.

It is very important not to overcook the omelette and let it become dry, and that is why the watercress filling should be added while there is still some un-cooked mixture left. By the time you come to serve it, the egg will have set, and even if it hasn't, you'll find the little bit of moisture rather pleasing.

If you want to make the watercress filling ahead of cooking the omelette, warm the watercress through gently for a few minutes before transferring it to the omelette. Such a large omelette calls for a large (about 12 inch/30 cm diameter) frying-pan; if you do not possess one, make two smaller omelettes, dividing the filling between them.

Preparation time: 15–20 minutes
Cooking time: 15 minutes

For Four Helpings:
3 bunches (4 oz/115 g each) of fresh watercress
2 oz/55 g butter
½ tsp salt

2 oz/55 g butter
8 eggs
2 tbs water
1 tsp salt
pepper

1 First prepare the watercress: separate the leaves from the stalks (don't worry if you leave some of the thin ones attached) and discard the stalks. Wash it.
2 Keep back 2 tbs of the leaves for decoration and put the remainder in the saucepan with the first 2 oz/55 g of butter.
3 Add the salt and pepper but NO liquid (the salt will make the watercress water a little) and set it, covered, over a gentle flame. Stirring from time to time, let it simmer for 10 minutes. By then the watercress should be a tender dark green mass but it should not have lost its piquant freshness. Remove from the heat and set aside in a warm place.
4 Break the 8 eggs into a bowl, add the water (it makes the mixture lighter), some salt and pepper and whisk to a homogeneous froth.
5 Melt the remaining butter in a large frying-pan, making sure that it spreads out evenly. When it is beginning to foam, pour in the egg mixture. The edges and middle will cook first; as they become set, move them with a spatula so that more of the liquid can reach these places. This operation will take about 5 minutes over a moderate flame.
6 When there are patches of unset omelette left, add the watercress, forming a green band dividing the omelette in half, and then roll it up. Scatter over the remaining watercress leaves.

VARIATION
4–6 oz/115–170 g cooked spinach can be used as a filling instead of the watercress.

POTATO PIE

A green vegetable such as broccoli, peas or beans looks pretty with the pie. Strong, young red wine, cider or bitter suits this country-style dish.

Preparation time: 20–25 minutes
Cooking time: 60–70 minutes

For Five to Six Helpings:
2½ lb/1.1 kg potatoes
1 green pepper
1 red pepper

FOR THE SAUCE:
1 onion
2 cloves of garlic
2 oz/55 g butter
1½ oz/40 g flour
1 pt/570 ml milk
2 tsp salt
freshly ground black pepper

FOR THE PASTRY:
6 oz/170 g plain flour
3 oz/85 g soft (i.e. room temperature) butter
1 tsp salt
2–3 tbs cold water

nob of butter
few tbs of flour for rolling out the pastry
6 tbs watercress or fresh coriander leaf for a piquant garnish

1   Set the oven to Reg. 4 (350°F, 175°C).
2   Grease a very large pie dish (or roasting tin).
3   Now prepare the pastry. Tip the flour into a bowl and to it add the butter and salt. Cut the butter into small nuggets and then let your fingers reduce them to tiny pieces so that they mix with the flour completely. You can check to see whether this has been achieved by shaking the bowl and observing whether any fat rises to the surface; if it does, 'rub' it in.
4   Add the cold water and stir it in to bind the mixture. Scatter some flour on a clean surface and on it roll out the pastry to a piece about 1 inch/2 cm larger than the diameter of the pie dish.
5   Peel and chop the onion and garlic finely.
6   To make the sauce, first melt the butter in a pan and in it cook the onion and garlic for a few minutes, without letting them brown. Stir in the flour to form a roux. Then, very slowly at first, start adding the milk, stirring the mixture all the time so that you form a lump-free sauce. Bring to the boil and add the seasoning.
7   Remove the seeds from the peppers and chop them roughly. Peel the potatoes and then cut them into slices no thicker than 50p coins.
8   Lay the potatoes in the dish, mix in the pepper and then pour over the sauce. Lay the pastry on top. Prick it in half a dozen places, press down the sides and then transfer the pie to the middle of the oven and leave it to cook for an hour. It is ready when the pastry has gently bronzed.

See also:
Tagliatelle with mushrooms p. 78.
Mixed fried rice p. 79.
Goats' cheese toasts p. 22.
Mushroom quiche p. 28.
Ham (replace with cheese or bean curd) and bean sprouts p. 71.
Recipes in vegetable and salads p. 95–104.

Vegetables and salads

Vegetables and salads

Please buy only fresh vegetables: they taste so much better than their frozen counterparts and are often cheaper. In the following table I have set out the main points about buying, preparing and boiling vegetables to accompany cooked dishes, and there are a few notes on which ones are good to eat raw. I have not included those that are difficult to obtain nor those, such as aubergines, that require much more preparation to make them enjoyable, and virtually become a meal on their own. Nevertheless, there follow some more elaborate treatments, and then salads.

The quantities in the table are the amounts you will need if you are serving only one vegetable; if you settle on two, simply halve them. You will see that the quantities to buy per helping vary considerably; this is because the amount of waste, such as the pods of peas, is different for different vegetables; for example, much of a cabbage is not used but hardly anything needs to be discarded from mange-touts or many kinds of beans.

With the exception of potatoes, all vegetables should be cooked in a very small amount of water so that they are only half covered and thus are partially steamed (or simply use a steamer). This will ensure that you don't lose all the flavours (and nutrients) to the cooking water which is later drained off (though it is worth keeping for making soups and sauces). Most vegetables should be added to boiling salted water as I have indicated, and the pan should be covered during the cooking.

The quantity of salt to add will vary with personal taste but I think a good guide is to allow ¼–½ tsp per helping. You will just have to discover what you like, and it's worth doing this because salt added afterwards gives a different and less satisfactory result.

Vegetable	Time of Year in Season	Quantity to Buy per Helping oz/g	Preparation	Cooking	Serving	Other Notes
Asparagus	May–June	5–7 oz/ 140–200 g	With a knife or vegetable peeler scrape the shoot beneath the (green) tip. Cut off the earthy end. Tie in bunches and lay flat in a saucepan; cover with lightly salted water.	Boil 12–15 minutes.	Drain off the water and transfer shoots to a warm dish. Remove string. Serve melted butter separately.	Whole asparagus makes a delicious first course. The tips can be served as a vegetable; they are very good but it's fairly extravagant as you need to allow more like 10–12 oz/285–340 g of unprepared shoots per person.
Beans Broad	May–Sept	8–12 oz/ 225–340 g (There is a lot of wastage)	Remove beans from their pods.	Add beans to salted boiling water. Simmer 5–8 minutes.	Drain and add a nob of butter and salt and pepper to taste.	If the beans are long (and old), remove the white skins before serving them. It is easiest to do this when they are cold, so you will need to re-heat them later with some butter.
Beans French	All year (but expensive in winter)	3–4 oz/ 85–115 g	Top and tail and wash.	Add to boiling salted water. Cook 8–10 minutes.	Drain; add butter and seasoning to taste.	If the beans are old remove the 'strings' from their long edges before cooking.
Beans Runner	July–Sept	4–5 oz/ 115–140g	Top and tail, slice and wash.	Add to boiling salted water. Simmer 5–8 minutes.	Drain; add butter and seasoning.	Remove the 'strings' if the beans are on the large side and look old.
Broccoli	All year	4–6 oz/ 115–170 g	Cut off thick ends of stalks and wash.	Add to boiling salted water. Boil 5–8 minutes.	Drain; add butter and seasoning.	There are two types commonly available, the indigenous kind with small florets (white, green or purple) and the Italian large-headed compact type known as calabrese.
Brussels Sprouts	Sept–March	6–8 oz/ 170–225 g	Remove outer leaves and stalks. Cut an X in base and wash.	Add to boiling salted water. Simmer 5–8 minutes.	Drain off water; add a nob of butter and seasoning.	See p. 100 for Brussels sprouts with walnuts.
Cabbage (green)	All year	4–8 oz/ 115–225 g (See Notes)	Remove outer leaves, quarter, core and slice. Wash.	Add to boiling salted water. Boil 5–6 minutes.	Drain; add butter and salt and pepper.	There are many different types of green cabbage; different varieties are in season at different times of the year. The amount of waste depends on the variety; for example, much less of a Savoy is discarded than of a

Vegetable	Time of Year in Season	Quantity to Buy per Helping oz/g	Preparation	Cooking	Serving	Other Notes
Cabbage (green) continued						spring cabbage. Look at them before buying to help you decide how much you will need.
Cabbage (white)	All year	4–6 oz/ 115–170 g	Remove outer leaves, quarter, core and slice. Wash.	Add to boiling salted water. Boil 5 minutes.	Drain; add butter and seasoning.	Often used raw in salads.
Carrots	All year	3–5 oz/ 85–140 g	Peel, top and tail, and slice (or leave whole).	Add to boiling salted water. Boil 8–12 minutes.	Drain; add butter, seasoning and chopped parsley.	New carrots often don't need peeling – just washing. They are delicious raw too. See p. 99 for carrots in dill sauce.
Cauliflower	All year	6–10 oz/ 170–285 g	Cut up into florets and wash.	Add to boiling salted water. Boil 6–8 minutes.	Drain; add butter and seasoning.	See p. 100 for cauliflower with almonds. It's so good when it's not overcooked, and some like it raw.
Chicory	Most of year	4–6 oz/ 115–170 g	Remove outer leaves and base and then slice. Wash.	Add to small amount of boiling salted water to which a little butter has been added. Boil 1–2 minutes.	Drain off water. A dusting of parsley looks pretty.	Many people love the slight bitterness when used raw in salads.
Courgettes (Baby marrows)	All year	6–8 oz/ 170–225 g	Top, tail, slice and wash.	Add to boiling salted water. Boil 5–8 minutes.	Drain and add plenty of butter.	Alternatively they can be simply fried in olive oil and butter. See p. 99 for courgettes and herbs recipe. They can be used raw in salads as an alternative to cucumber.
Fennel	All year	4–6 oz/ 115–170 g	Peel off outer layer, cut off stem and wash. Quarter, core and slice roughly.	Add to boiling salted water. Boil 5–8 minutes.	Drain off water; add butter and salt and pepper to taste.	Fennel has a strong flavour. It is good mixed with other vegetables such as carrots, broccoli or mange-touts. It is delicious raw in salads.
Leeks	August– May	6–8 oz/ 170–225 g	Remove outer one or two layers, earthy base and green tops. Slice and wash.	Add leeks to boiling salted water. Cooking time 5–8 minutes.	Drain; add salt and pepper and butter to taste.	

Vegetable	Time of Year in Season	Quantity to Buy per Helping oz/g	Preparation	Cooking	Serving	Other Notes
Mange-touts	All year (expensive)	3–4 oz/ 85–115 g	Top and tail and wash.	Add them to boiling salted water and boil 5–6 minutes.	Drain; add butter and seasoning to taste.	These can also be used cold (cooked or raw) in salads very successfully.
Mushrooms	All year	4–6 oz/ 115–170 g	Remove stalks and wash or peel.	Sauté in a little butter with salt and pepper for 5–10 minutes.	Serve in cooking juices.	The large flat mushrooms, now widely available, have flavour; button mushrooms rarely do but are popular because they do not release brown juices. Wild ones found in fields have the best flavour of all, but make sure they are proper mushrooms. They are good raw.
Peas	June– Sept	6–8 oz/ 170–225 g	Remove from pods.	Add peas to boiling salted water. Boil 3–5 minutes.	Drain; add butter and seasoning to taste.	A sprig of mint, in the cooking water, imparts a pleasant flavour.
Potatoes	All year	4–8 oz/ 115–225 g (depends on appetite)	Scrub or peel and cut up any large ones so they are all same size (so they will cook in same time) and wash. Put in pan of cold salted water.	Bring to boil. Cooking time 10–20 minutes.	Drain; add butter and seasoning.	A sprig of mint, added during or after the cooking, is good with potatoes – particularly new ones. See p. 102 for instructions on baking potatoes, and p. 101 for other potato recipes.
Spinach	Most of year	6–8 oz/ 170–225 g	Remove stalks and wash.	Cook the spinach with very little salted water. Boiling time: 3–5 minutes.	Drain very thoroughly. Add butter, salt and pepper to taste.	Spinach beet, which is very similar to true spinach, is a good substitute. See p. 102 for spinach dressed with cream and cumin. Young tender spinach is good raw.

CARROTS IN A CREAMY DILL SAUCE

The bright orange of the carrots is set off beautifully by the green speckled sauce. Serve carrots prepared in this way either hot with, for example, roast lamb or beef or as part of a cold spread; they go very well with cold salmon trout (see p. 40). If you wish to serve them cold, put them in the fridge after step 5 and leave them for several hours.

Preparation time: 5–10 minutes
Cooking time: 10–15 minutes

For Six Helpings:
2 lb/905 g carrots
1/2 pt/285 ml water
2 tsp salt
freshly ground pepper
1/2 pt/285 ml single cream
2 tsp dried dill weed or 2 tbs fresh dill weed

1 Peel the carrots, and top and tail them. If they are on the fat side, slice them in half lengthways, trying to ensure that they are all approximately the same width so that they will cook in an equal time.
2 Bring the salted water to the boil and then cook the carrots for 8–12 minutes (the exact time will depend on their thickness) so that they are just tender, not mushy.
3 If you are using fresh dill weed, chop it finely now.
4 Strain the water from the carrots and put them in a warm covered serving dish. Pour the cream into a pan, add plenty of pepper and the dill weed and mix together.
5 Taste the sauce, adjust the seasoning if necessary, bring briefly to the boil and then immediately pour over the carrots.

AROMATIC COURGETTES

In this recipe the courgettes are first lightly boiled and then added to some butter and oil; this reduces the amount of fat used in the cooking. Courgettes cooked in this fashion go nicely with haddock.

Preparation time: 10–15 minutes
Cooking time: 8–12 minutes

For Six Helpings:
2½–3 lb/1.1–1.35 kg courgettes
2 pt/1.1 l water
1 dsp salt
3 cloves garlic
1 oz/30 g butter
2 tbs olive oil
1 dsp dried basil
pepper

1 Set the salted water to boil. Wash the courgettes, top and tail them and then slice them into rounds about an inch/2 cm long. Boil the courgettes for 6–10 minutes.
2 Meanwhile peel and chop the garlic finely.
3 The courgettes are ready when they are tender but still firm. Drain the water from them.
4 Put the butter and oil in a saucepan and when it is warm add the garlic and fry for a minute or two, but do not brown.
5 Add the courgettes, the basil, some ground pepper and salt (if necessary) and stir all together over a moderate heat for a couple of minutes.

BRUSSELS SPROUTS WITH WALNUTS

One day I took on preparing a whole heap of fresh chestnuts so I could serve them with Brussels sprouts. It was an enormous labour scoring their skins, boiling them, then nearly burning my fingers as I tried to remove the skins and finally finding many were rotten inside. Never again, I said. Walnuts can be bought ready shelled, so you can see if there are any bad ones, and to my mind they offer a more interesting addition to the sprouts than chestnuts. They make an excellent accompaniment to any roast meat.

Preparation time: 10–15 minutes
Cooking time: 8–10 minutes

For Six Helpings:
3 lb/1.35 kg Brussels sprouts
1½ pt/850 ml water
3 tsp salt
1 oz/30 g butter
4 oz/115 g shelled walnut pieces

1　Put the salted water on to boil. Meanwhile remove the outer leaves from the sprouts and their stalks. Cut a cross in the base. Wash them.
2　Cook the sprouts for 5–8 minutes. They are ready when a sharp knife just cuts through them easily. Try not to let them become soft.
3　Drain the water from the sprouts and put them in a warm covered serving bowl.
4　Melt the butter in a saucepan and then add the walnut pieces. Cook for a minute or two to crisp them up and then add the cooked sprouts and some pepper.

CAULIFLOWER WITH ALMONDS

A good way to dress up cauliflower. This dish goes well with chicken and meat roasts, and even some fish, e.g. cod or haddock.

Preparation time: 5–10 minutes
Cooking time: 8–10 minutes

For Six Helpings:
2 medium-size cauliflowers
1 pt/570 ml water
2–3 tsp salt
3 oz/85 g blanched split almonds
1 oz/30 g butter
pepper

1　Set the salted water on to boil. Meanwhile cut the cauliflower into florets and wash.
2　Simmer the cauliflower for about five minutes; it should retain a hint of crunchiness. Chop the almonds roughly.
3　Drain the water from the cauliflower, put it in a serving dish and cover.
4　Melt the butter in a frying-pan, add the almonds and fry together over a good heat for several minutes to brown the almonds gently. Then scatter over the cauliflower.

GENOAN POTATOES

My husband very much enjoyed potatoes cooked in this fashion when he visited Genoa.

Preparation time: 10–15 minutes
Cooking time: about 1 hour

For Six Helpings:
2½–3 lb/1.1–1.35 kg potatoes
3 cloves garlic
2–3 tsp salt
pepper
¾ pt/425 ml milk
½ oz/15 g butter

1 Set the oven to Reg. 6 (400°F, 205°C). Grease a pie dish with a little of the butter.
2 Peel the potatoes and chop them into pieces the size of large button mushrooms. Peel and chop the garlic finely.
3 Lay the potatoes, with the garlic and seasoning, in the dish and pour over the milk. Dot the surface with the remainder of the butter and cover.
4 Cook the potatoes in the top part of the oven for one hour. By this time they should be quite soft.

MASHED POTATOES AND DILL

This makes an excellent accompaniment to grilled fish.

Preparation time: 10–15 minutes
Cooking time: 15–20 minutes

For Six Helpings:
2½–3 lb/1.1–1.35 kg old potatoes
sufficient water to cover them
3 tsp salt
3–4 tsp dried dill weed or 3–4 tbs fresh dill weed
3 oz/85 g butter
6 tbs single cream
salt and pepper to taste

1 Peel the potatoes and cut them up if necessary so they are all the same size (this will ensure they all cook in the same time). Drop them into the saucepan and cover with water. Add the salt and boil for about 15 minutes, when they should cut very easily.
2 If you are using fresh dill weed, chop it up finely.
3 Drain the water from the potatoes, and away from the heat, add the butter and cream and mash them.
4 Add the dill, salt and pepper to taste and mix together.

BAKED POTATOES WITH CARDAMOM SAUCE

Preparation time: 10–15 minutes
Cooking time: 45–60 minutes

For Six Helpings:
6 baking potatoes
1 tbs salt

FOR THE SAUCE:
1 clove garlic
½ small onion
5 green pods of cardamom
1½ oz/40 g butter
1 oz/30 g flour
½ pt/285 ml milk
½–1 tsp salt
pepper
2 tbs single cream

1　Heat the oven at Reg. 5 (375°F, 190°C) for 10 minutes. Wash the potatoes, removing any blemishes, and then roll them in salt. Put them in the oven for 45–60 minutes.
2　To make the sauce, first peel and chop the onion and garlic finely. Remove the cardamom from its pods and crush the seeds.
3　Fry the onion and garlic in the butter for a few minutes, without letting them brown.
4　Add the flour and then very slowly add the milk so that you form a smooth sauce.
5　Stir in the cardamom, salt and pepper; taste and adjust the seasoning if necessary. Coat the sauce with the cream to prevent a skin forming and re-heat it when the potatoes are done.

SPINACH MIRANDA

This complements any fish or meat dish.

Preparation time: 10–15 minutes
Cooking time: 10–12 minutes

For Six Helpings:
2 lb/905 g fresh spinach
½ pt/285 ml water
2–3 tsp salt
½ pt/285 ml single cream
2 tsp ground cumin
freshly ground pepper

1　Wash the spinach and remove the stalks.
2　Boil the salted water in a large pan and to it add the spinach. Cook for 5–8 minutes.
3　Drain the spinach through a colander and press out all the water.
4　Pour the cream into the pan, add the cumin and some pepper and bring to the boil.
5　Stir the spinach into the sauce, taste and adjust the seasoning if necessary.

CUCUMBER AND AVOCADO SALAD

Preparation time: 5–10 minutes

For Six Helpings:
1 cucumber
2 ripe avocados
6 tbs fresh coriander leaves
2 tsp salt
freshly ground pepper

FOR THE DRESSING:
4 tbs olive oil
1 tbs lemon juice

1   Peel the cucumber, if you wish, and then slice it thinly and arrange it on a flat plate. Peel the avocados and slice them over the cucumber.
2   Scatter over the coriander leaves, then the seasoning and finally the dressing.

WINTER SALAD

Preparation time: 5–10 minutes

For Six to Eight Helpings:
1 endive (curly and lettuce-like)
8 oz/225 g bean sprouts
3 carrots
2 tsp salt
freshly ground pepper

FOR THE DRESSING:
¼ pt/140 ml olive oil
2 tbs lemon/lime juice
½ tsp French mustard

1   Remove the outer leaves from the endive and then wash the paler green ones thoroughly and then dry them.
2   Peel the carrots and then slice them, lengthways, into paper-thin slivers.
3   Mix the dressing ingredients together in the bottom of a large salad bowl.
4   Throw the endive, carrots and bean sprouts on top of the dressing. Add salt and pepper and toss the salad.

BULGHUR AND MINT SALAD

Bulghur is a kind of wheat that has been cracked and partially cooked, and so a short soaking is all it needs to turn it into an interesting salad ingredient. It is fairly filling, so a little goes a long way. Most health food shops stock it. The salad is often known as tabbouleh.

Preparation time: 5–10 minutes
Soaking time: 1 hour

For Six Helpings:
9 oz/255 g bulghur
¾ pt/425 ml water
1 small onion
1 oz/30 g fresh mint leaves
1 oz/30 g parsley
2 tbs olive oil
2–3 tsp salt
freshly ground pepper

1 Mix the bulghur with the water and leave to stand for an hour.
2 Peel and dice the onion.
3 Remove the mint and parsley from their stems and chop the leaves finely.
4 Strain the bulghur through a sieve, being sure to remove all the excess water.
5 Return the bulghur to the bowl, along with the onion and herbs.
6 Stir in the olive oil and season to taste.

SALAD OF PASTA

Here is a recipe for a warm salad.

Preparation time: 10–15 minutes
Cooking time: 10–12 minutes

For Six to Eight Helpings:
12 oz/340 g dried pasta such as bows, quills, shells or gnocchi
3½–4 pt/2–2.3 l water
3 tsp salt
8 oz/225 g watercress
1 red pepper
4 oz/115 g walnut pieces
6 tbs olive oil
1–2 tsp salt
pepper

1 Boil the pasta in the salted water for 10–12 minutes. Drain off the water.
2 While the pasta is cooking, remove the seeds from the pepper and dice it roughly. Remove the big stalks from the watercress.
3 Pour the olive oil into a bowl, and into it turn the pasta, pepper, watercress, walnuts, salt and pepper. Taste and adjust the seasoning if necessary.

Puddings

Puddings

Most of the recipes here are for cold puddings but nevertheless they often need some cooking during their evolution – for example, Mollon's Peaches and Bananas in Plum Sauce. Besides these very simple treatments there are three culinary 'building blocks' for puddings: egg custards, pastry and meringue. Real egg custards, with plenty of brandy, are the ingredients that make a successful trifle, and it is an egg custard of a kind that bathes the ratafias in the chocolate and ratafia pudding. Ice-cream too begins with an egg custard, to which is added some meringue, to make it light and not too hard even when it is very cold. The pastry concoctions are more obvious: tarts and apple crumble – the crumble is just pastry without its water. There are no special 'do's and don'ts' of the pudding art; just be sure to enjoy making and eating them.

FRUIT SALAD

The great thing about fruit salad is for it to taste fresh; try not to make it many hours before it will be consumed because then it will become a sad and limp dish. It will keep in the fridge for 2–3 hours but if you do this remember to take it out about half an hour before serving so that the flavours have a chance to come out, and only then peel the bananas and add them, otherwise they will have turned brown. The other secret is to buy the best-quality fruit – in a dish as simple as this, the quality of the raw ingredients will inevitably show through. Your labour will be slight, so be generous in your purchases.

Obviously the composition will vary with your mood and the time of year. I'll give a summer and then a winter version but both are really just suggestions and no doubt you'll develop your own variations after a while. Serve the fruit salad with cream, whipped or not, and plain biscuits, such as *langues de chat* or sponge fingers, or with meringues. A glass of sweet white wine will not go amiss.

First, the summer recipe.

Preparation time: 15–20 minutes

For Six Helpings:
12 oz/340 g strawberries or raspberries
8 oz/225 g grapes (preferably seedless)
4 ripe nectarines or peaches
3 bananas

1 Remove the husks from the soft fruit. (Try to resist the temptation to wash the fruit; it will only make it go soft.)
2 Remove the seeds from the grapes if you have been unable to buy seedless ones.
3 Peel and slice the nectarines or peaches. Peel the bananas and cut in half lengthways.
4 Arrange the fruit in a pretty pattern on a large flat plate.

Now the winter version:

For Six Helpings:
2 satsumas (or 1 orange)
1 small pineapple (or ½ large one)
8 oz/225 g grapes (preferably seedless)
3 bananas
2 kiwi fruits or 6 lychees

1 Peel the satsumas or orange and divide up, being careful to remove all the white pith.
2 Cut the outside off the pineapple, slice into quarters, remove the inner core and then dice.
3 Remove the seeds from the grapes if you have been unable to buy seedless ones.
4 Peel and slice the kiwi fruit or peel the lychees. Peel the bananas, and slice lengthways.
5 Arrange the fruit on a large platter.

VARIATION
Frozen raspberries, if you can buy them, make a nice addition to the winter salad. They will need several hours in which to thaw. Frozen strawberries are no good – they lose their shape, texture and colour on freezing.

BANANA ISLANDS IN PLUM SAUCE

The pale banana slices look very good in their deep purple plum sea, and the flavours set each other off nicely. Serve the pudding with lashings of thick cream and, if possible, almond meringues (see p.132). The purée can be made the day before it is needed.

Preparation time: 10–15 minutes
Cooking time: 5 minutes
Cooling time: at least 2 hours

For Six Helpings:
2½ lb/1.1 kg cooking plums
8 oz/225 g caster sugar (this quantity is for very tart cooking plums; if yours are sweeter, use less sugar)
2 tbs water
6 bananas

1 There's no need to peel the plums but you should remove their stones by cutting them in half longitudinally and picking out the stone with a sharp knife. Put the plum halves in a large saucepan as you go along.

2 Add the sugar and the water, cover and set the plums to boil gently, stirring occasionally, for about 10 minutes. By the end of this time they should be a soft mass.

3 Remove the saucepan from the heat, transfer the mixture to an electric blender and blend it to a purée (or put it through a sieve).

4 Turn the purée into a serving dish and put it in the fridge for at least 2 hours.

5 Peel and slice the bananas into pieces about ½ inch/1 cm thick. (Do not do this earlier because banana tends to turn a rather unappetizing brown colour.) Stir them into the plum purée.

VARIATIONS

Banana islands in gooseberry sauce (always known in my family as 'Pond Life') are also good. For six helpings substitute 2½ lb/1.1 kg gooseberries for the plums in the above recipe. Top, tail and wash them and then proceed as above. Blackcurrants make a pretty background to the banana pieces, and for six helpings substitute 2½ lb/1.1 kg blackcurrants for the plums. Remove their stalks and wash and then go on as usual.

APPASSIONATA

A deliciously light, creamy cold pudding. It is very easy to make and can be made the day before it is needed. Sauternes or any other kind of sweet white wine is a joy to drink with it.

It is important to add the meringues at the very last minute so that they remain crisp and crunchy. Steps 1 and 2 may be carried out in advance.

Preparation time: 5–10 minutes

For Six Helpings:
¾ pt/425 ml double cream
2 oz/55 g icing sugar
10 passionfruits (ripe ones have wrinkled skins)
6 meringues

1 Pour the cream into a bowl and whisk until it is thick but not stiff. Stir in the icing sugar.
2 Cut the passionfruits in half and, taking each half in turn, squeeze the juice and seeds into the cream.
3 Just before serving, crumble the meringues into pieces into a serving bowl. Stir in the cream mixture.

VARIATION
This pudding is also good ice cold. Follow steps 1 and 2 as above and add the crumbled meringues, then turn the mixture into a small cake tin (with a removable base) and put in the freezer for at least 2 hours. About half an hour before you wish to eat it, remove it to the fridge. Lift the 'cake' from the tin and slip onto a plate to serve.

BAKED APPLES

An old English favourite. Serve the hot apples by themselves or with cream. If you are feeling energetic, you could accompany them with egg custard (see p.112 for recipe).

Preparation time: 10–15 minutes
Cooking time: 30–40 minutes

For Six Helpings:
6 largish cooking apples, each weighing
6–8 oz/170–225 g (Bramleys are the best)
2 oz/55 g butter
6 tbs honey
6 oz/170 g seedless raisins
¼ pt/140 ml water

1 Switch on the oven to Reg. 4 (350°F, 175°C).
2 Butter the bottom and sides of an ovenproof dish with a little of the butter.
3 Core the apples and fill each with raisins, packing them in tightly. Scatter the rest around the apples.
4 Heap a spoonful of honey on each apple and divide the remainder of the butter in six and top each with it. Pour round the water.
5 Put the dish in the middle of the hot oven.
6 The apples will take about 35 minutes to cook – they are ready when a knife goes into them easily. They may split their skins – don't worry about this. They will keep in the turned-off oven quite happily for up to half an hour.

MOLLON'S PEACHES

The first time I prepared this combination of lightly baked peaches served with cardamom-flavoured cream I gave it to some scientist friends of my husband's. One of them, the colour-vision expert John Mollon, was quite spell-bound by the pudding, and so it seemed right to name the dish after its first and finest taster. It should be eaten cold.

Preparation time: 15–20 minutes
Cooking time: 25–30 minutes
Cooling time: 2 hours

For Six Helpings:
6 large ripe peaches
2 tbs caster sugar
optional: **2 tbs desiccated coconut**
nob of butter

FOR THE CREAM:
6 green pods of cardamom
2 dsp caster sugar
2 dsp water
½ pt/285 ml double cream

1 Set the oven to Reg. 4 (350°F, 175°C).
2 Peel the peaches. If this proves troublesome, set a pan of water on to boil. When it is simmering, drop in the peaches, three at a time, and leave them in the water for half a minute. Then remove them and skin them, which should now be easy. Halve the peaches.
3 Use the nob of butter to grease an ovenproof dish lightly and then lay the peaches in it.
4 If you like coconut, sprinkle it over the fruit, and then the sugar.
5 Set the peaches to cook in the oven for 25 minutes, when they should be tender if pierced with a sharp knife. (If they aren't ready, give them 5–10 min-

utes longer.) Remove them from the oven and put them in a fridge or cold place for a couple of hours.
6 While the peaches are baking, prepare the cream. Crush the cardamom pods. (If you don't have a pestle and mortar, crush them on a board or plate with a knife). Now put the sugar, water and cardamom in a small saucepan and dissolve the sugar over moderate heat. Stir from time to time and then bring the syrup to the boil for a couple of minutes. Remove it from the heat.
7 Pour the cream into a bowl and whisk it up so that it forms soft peaks and is snow-like.
8 Pour the syrup through a sieve or strainer into the cream and lightly whisk again. Keep the cream in the fridge until you are ready to serve it with the peaches.

EGG CUSTARD
(crème anglaise):

Preparation time: 5–10 minutes
Cooking time: 5–10 minutes

For Six Helpings:
1 pt/570 ml milk
5 egg yolks (to separate eggs, juggle the yolks between the shells as you pour off the whites)
3 oz/85 g caster sugar
½ tsp plain flour*

1   Whisk the sugar into the yolks and then beat together for a few minutes. Add the flour.
2   Put the milk in a saucepan and bring it to the boil. Remove it from the heat and pour it on to the egg mixture SLOWLY, beating all the time.
3   Return the custard to the pan and, over a low heat, stir it with a wooden spoon; don't on any account let it boil. It should thicken slightly, and it is ready when it coats the back of a wooden spoon.
4   Draw it away from the heat and beat it a little to cool it down if you are going to leave it in the pan, or pour it into a very slightly warmed jug. It will keep warm for about ½ hour if you stand it by the cooker – not on it.

*   The addition of the small amount of flour helps prevent the egg yolks in the custard curdling but even so you need to be careful not to overheat the liquid. I think it's very difficult to detect the flour but purists may say it's wrong to add it.

GOOSEBERRY SORBET

This sorbet is rather like an iced gooseberry fool. It has the strange property of tasting creamy and yet contains no cream; this quality is due to the beaten egg whites. Wafer-thin plain biscuits and some sweet white wine make good accompaniments.

Turn the fridge or freezer to its highest setting a couple of hours before making the sorbet, which will keep well for several days after you have made it.

Preparation time: 15–20 minutes
Cooking time: 5–10 minutes
Chilling time: 6–8 hours or overnight

For Six Helpings:
1 lb/455 g gooseberries
6 oz/170 g icing sugar
juice of 1 lemon
2 egg whites (separate the eggs by pouring off the whites as you juggle the yolks between the shells)

1   Top and tail the gooseberries and put them in a pan with the sugar (but no water).
2   Cover and simmer the gooseberries, stirring them from time to time, for 5–10 minutes until they are quite soft and pulp like.
3   Sieve the fruit or purée it and add the lemon juice.
4   Beat the egg whites until they form stiff peaks – as though you were making meringues – and then gently stir them into the gooseberries.
5   Put the sorbet mixture into the freezer and leave it to set. Look at it after a couple of hours and give it a stir. Thereafter you should try to mix the freezing purée together every hour until it is firm, so that the egg whites are incorporated properly and the sorbet is smooth and free of ice crystals.

APPLE CRUMBLE

Another traditional pudding – remember the apple crumble at school? This recipe was given to me by an old friend; it is very good. Because you use so much sugar in the crumble mixture, you don't need to add any to the fruit; nor do you need any liquid, because the sugar will encourage the apples to exude their own juices.

It may be served piping hot from the oven, warm or cold. Real egg custard (see p.112) goes well with the warm version, and cream or yogurt with the cold crumble. Some may like a dusting of brown sugar too.

Preparation time: 10–15 minutes
Cooking time: 1½–2 hours

For Six Helpings:
6 oz/170 g plain flour
4 oz/115 g unsalted butter (at room temperature)
5 oz/140 g caster sugar

2½ lb/1.1 kg Bramley or other good tart cooking apples
optional: **1 tsp ground cinnamon**
nob of butter for greasing the dish

1   Set the oven to Reg. 4 (350°F, 175°C).
2   Start with the crumble mixture. Put the flour in the mixing bowl and then the butter. Cut through the butter with a knife so that you reduce it to nut-size pieces.
3   Now use your fingers to break the butter into even tinier pieces. Using one, or both hands, rub a little of the mixture gently between your fingers and thumb. As it drops down into the bowl, take another bit and carry on like this until you can't see the butter pieces any more. You can test how successful you've been by shaking the bowl for a few seconds and looking to see whether any butter pieces rise to the surface. If some are left, rub them in. Stir in the sugar.

4   Grease an ovenproof dish with butter.
5   Peel the apples and then cut the fruit into 50p thick slices straight into the dish. Discard the cores.
6   Stir the ground cinnamon into the apple slices if you so desire.
7   Tip the crumble mixture over the apples, smooth the surface and transfer the dish to the middle of the oven.
8   Leave the crumble to cook for 1½ hours. By the end of this time the top should be nicely browned and the apples underneath soft and tender. Give the pudding another ½ hour if you think the crumble should be a more golden brown.

WALNUT ICE-CREAM

This is good on its own or, perhaps a little surprisingly, with a fruit pudding. Hot ginger sauce (see recipe opposite) makes a good spicy accompaniment to the nutty ice-cream.

Turn the freezer up to its highest setting a couple of hours before making the ice-cream.

Preparation time: 10–15 minutes
Cooking time: 5–10 minutes
Freezing time: 5–6 hours or overnight

For Six Helpings:
4 oz/115 g walnut pieces
¾ pt/425 ml double cream
4 eggs
5 oz/140 g icing sugar
½ tsp flour

1   Set the oven to Reg. 5 (375° F, 190°C).
2   Separate the eggs by juggling the yolks between the shells as you pour off the whites into one bowl, and accumulate the yolks in another.
3   Beat the icing sugar into the yolks and then stir in the flour.
4   Scatter the walnuts over a baking tray and slide them into the oven to brown for 5–10 minutes.
5   Pour the cream into a saucepan, bring it to the boil and then whisk it into the egg-yolk mixture.
6   Return the creamy custard to the saucepan and, stirring all the time, cook it over a gentle heat. It should thicken as the egg yolks and flour cook – but do not let it boil on any account. Remove the pan from the heat as soon as the yellow mixture coats the back of the spoon and it is too hot for your finger. Pour it through a sieve (to remove any curdled bits of egg) back into the bowl.
7   By now the walnuts should be browned, so pulverize them in a liquidizer or food processor and then stir them into the custard.
8   Whisk the egg whites until they are stiff and then stir them in too.
9   Put the mixture in the freezer and leave it to cool. After a couple of hours the mixture nearest the sides of the dish should begin to freeze, so give it a stir. If you want to make smooth, crystal-free ice-cream, you will need to whisk the mixture up once an hour for the next few hours until it has all frozen. (It will not become rock hard because the egg whites help to keep it soft.)

GINGER SAUCE

Preparation time: 2–3 minutes
Cooking time: 5 minutes

For Six Helpings:
4 heaped tbs ginger preserve/marmalade
2 tbs water

Put the preserve and water into a pan and, mixing
them together, bring the concoction to the boil.

CHOCOLATE AND RATAFIA PUDDING

Serve this luscious pudding by itself after a fairly light main course or, if you're feeling very greedy, with cream.

It helps if you use really good-quality, very dark, bitter chocolate in the pudding, even though it then has sugar added to it. You might think it easier (and in line with the principles of this book) just to use sweeter milk chocolate but bitter chocolate has a truer chocolate flavour because fewer other flavours, such as vanilla, are added to it.

The pudding needs to be made the day before it is to be eaten.

Preparation time: 10–15 minutes
Cooking time: 5–10 minutes

For Six Helpings:
10 oz/285 g ratafias (or about 8 macaroons)
6 oz/170 g unsalted butter
6 oz/170 g caster sugar
2 egg yolks
10 oz/285 g very dark bitter chocolate
¼ pt/140 ml milk
4 tbs brandy or rum
grated rind of 2 oranges

1 Put the egg yolks in a mixing bowl and beat in the liquor and orange peel.
2 Melt the butter, with the chocolate, milk and sugar in a saucepan over a gentle heat. Stir the mixture from time to time to make a smooth, homogeneous cream. You need to watch it quite carefully to ensure the chocolate doesn't burn on the bottom of the pan.
3 Bring to the boil and immediately pour it over the egg yolk mixture SLOWLY, whisking all the time.
4 Continue beating for a few more minutes to cool it down a little – you don't want the egg yolks to curdle.
5 Put the ratafias in a serving bowl. (If you are using macaroons, crumble them up into ratafia-size pieces.)
6 Pour the chocolate cream over the biscuits, cover the dish and put it in the fridge or a cool place for a day.

BLACKCURRANT MERINGUE

The contrasting sharpness of the blackcurrants and smooth sweetness of the meringue (crisp on the outside, soft inside) makes this a very satisfying hot pudding, particularly after a rich meat course. It is easy and quick to prepare and should dispel your fears that meringue is difficult to make – it isn't. Serve the pudding by itself or with thick cream.

Preparation time: 15–20 minutes
Cooking time: 1½ hours

For Six Helpings:
2 lb/905 g blackcurrants
3 oz/85 g caster sugar

FOR THE MERINGUE:
6 egg whites (pour whites from the eggs while
 juggling the yolks between the shells)
12 oz/340 g caster sugar

1   Set the oven to Reg. 1 (300°F, 150°C).
2   First prepare the fruit. Remove the berries from their stalks and put them in a large (about 8 inch/ 20 cm diameter) ovenproof dish. Gently mix in the sugar.
3   Now make the meringue: put the egg whites in a large bowl and beat them until they form stiff peaks on the surface; it will take you about 2–3 minutes to achieve this with an electric beater and about 10 if you are using your own muscle power. Next sprinkle on the sugar and beat it in very quickly – for not longer than half a minute.
4   Pour the meringue over the fruit and put the bowl in the middle of the oven, leaving it to cook for 1½ hours. (By this time the top of the meringue should be nicely browned.)
   It will keep warm for ½–¾ hour in the turned-off oven.

PEARS IN RED WINE JELLY

Rather a pleasing alternative to the usual pears in red wine, it can be made the day before it is to be consumed. Serve the pears by themselves or with cream. Some plain biscuits make a nice accompaniment.

Preparation time: 15–20 minutes
Cooking time: 40–45 minutes
Setting time: 5–6 hours or overnight

For Six Helpings:
6 cooking pears (Conference are best) each
   weighing 4–6 oz/115–170 g
½ pt/285 ml water
½ pt/285 ml red wine
4 oz/115 g caster sugar
4 cloves
3 tsp powdered gelatine

1 Set the oven to Reg. 4 (350°F, 175°C).
2 Peel the pears.
3 Pour the water, wine and sugar into a large, ovenproof pan, and set it over moderate heat to dissolve the sugar.
4 Add the pears and cloves and bring to the boil.
5 Transfer the pot to the oven and let the pears cook for 40–45 minutes, when they should be tender. Remove from the oven.
6 Delicately lift the pears out of their cooking liquid and put them in a serving bowl.
7 Sprinkle the gelatine over the liquid, and dissolve it, over some heat, if necessary.
8 Remove the pan from the flame and pour half the liquid over the pears in the bowl and put it in the fridge to set. Keep the other half of the liquid out of the fridge. *
9 A couple of hours later, when the liquid in the bowl should have set, pour over the rest that you have kept back. (If it has turned a bit solid, gently melt it over a flame first.)
10 Return the bowl to the fridge to set the remainder of the jelly.

By preparing the jelly in this way, the pears become anchored in the first lot of liquid and then receive a red wine cover. If all the liquid were poured on at once, they would float to the top of the bowl and protrude from the surface of the jelly in a rather ungainly fashion.

BAKEWELL TART

Here is my version of this excellent Derbyshire pudding. It can be served warm or cold, with cream if you like.

Preparation time: 15–20 minutes
Cooking time: 45–50 minutes
Cooling time: 30 minutes or more

For Six to Eight Helpings:
FOR THE PASTRY:
3 oz/85 g room-temperature unsalted butter
5 oz/140 g plain flour
1 oz/30 g ground almonds
1 oz/30 g caster sugar
2 tbs cold water
nob of butter for greasing flan dish
few tbs flour on which to roll out the pastry

FOR THE FILLING:
3 level tbs raspberry jam
1 oz/30 g ground almonds
2 oz/55 g caster sugar
4 oz/115 g unsalted butter
2–3 drops almond essence
1 tbs milk
3 eggs
1 level tbs caster sugar
½ oz/15 g almond flakes

1 Set the oven to Reg. 6 (400°F, 205°C).
2 Grease the bottom and sides of a flan dish (about 9 inches/23 cm in diameter) with the nob of butter.
3 Put the butter, flour and ground almonds for the pastry in a bowl. Cut the butter into small pieces and then use your fingers to rub it in gently, so that it mixes in with the flour and almonds. Shake the bowl from time to time to see if any butter pieces rise to the surface; if they do, rub them in. Stir in the sugar.
4 Add the water and work it in gently with your hands; then transfer the pastry ball to a clean surface on which you have sprinkled some flour.
5 Roll the pastry out to a piece about an inch larger than the diameter of the bottom and sides of the dish.
6 Lay the pastry in the dish, press the sides in gently and let the extra pastry hang over the edges to allow for any shrinkage as it cooks. (You can remove the excess after the cooking if you wish – but it's nice to nibble.) Prick the bottom in a few places and then put the dish in the oven for 6–8 minutes.
7 Separate the eggs by juggling the yolks between the shells while pouring off the whites into a large bowl, and accumulate the yolks in another.
8 Remove the pastry shell from the oven and reduce the heat to Reg. 3 (325°F, 160°C).
9 Spread the jam over the pastry base.
10 Melt together the butter, sugar, ground almonds and almond essence in a large saucepan.
11 Remove the pan from the heat and beat in the milk and then the egg yolks, one at a time.
12 Whisk the egg whites up so that they form stiff peaks, sprinkle on the tablespoon of sugar and beat it in rapidly.
13 Stir one quarter of the egg whites into the almond mixture and fold in the remainder with a spatula: rotate the pan as you gently lift quantities of the almond mixture over the egg fluff. In no more than a couple of minutes the two should be fairly well incorporated (and as you pour the mixture onto the jam, it will mix up more.)
14 Pour the foam-like mixture into the dish, scatter over the almond flakes and put it in the middle of the oven for 30–35 minutes. By this time the top should have puffed (it will sink as it cools) and browned, and a knife plunged into the centre of the tart will come out clean.
15 Remove the tart from the oven and let it cool for about 30 minutes if you wish to serve it warm, or longer for a cold pudding.

GINGER RHUBARB TART

The Chinese have used both ginger and rhubarb in cooking and medicine for thousands of years, and so it seems right that the two should meet in cooking; here they do so in a cold tart.

You really need to make this tart the same day you are going to eat it because otherwise the rhubarb filling will make the pastry go soggy. A foolproof way of preventing this from happening is to paint the cooked pastry shell with melted redcurrant jelly using a pastry brush.

Cardamom cream (see p. 111) makes a delicious accompaniment to this tart, and so does a glass of sweet white wine, some marsala or Madeira.

Preparation time: 20–25 minutes
Cooking time: 50–60 minutes
Chilling time: 3–4 hours

For Six Helpings:
FOR THE PASTRY:
6 oz/170 g plain flour
3 oz/85 g unsalted butter at room temperature so it is fairly soft
1 oz/30 g caster sugar
2 tbs cold water
a couple of tbs flour for the rolling out

FOR THE FILLING:
1½ lb/680 g rhubarb – the young thin stalks are the best
3 heaped tbs ginger preserve or marmalade
2 oz/55 g sultanas
1½ tsp powdered gelatine

1 Turn the oven to Reg. 6 (400°F, 205°C).
2 Use a little of the butter to grease the bottom and sides of a flan dish (metal ones are best).
3 Sieve the flour into a bowl and to it add the butter. Cut the butter into nuggets and then use your fingers to 'rub' the fat into the flour gently. Draw it up through your fingers, squeezing it lightly, so that after a few minutes you have formed a homogeneous 'crumble' mixture. Check that all the butter pieces have been reduced in size by shaking the bowl for a few seconds. If there are any odd bits of butter left, they will come to the surface of the mixture; if this occurs, rub them in too. Add the sugar.
4 Now stir in the cold water and form the mixture in to a ball.
5 Scatter the other flour over a clean surface and then roll the pastry out on it. You will need to make a piece that is slightly larger than the bottom of your flan dish so there is sufficient to come up the sides and rest over the outside of the dish. (This is a safeguard against any shrinkage of the pastry that may occur as it cooks. Any excess can be cut off after the baking.)
6 Lay the pastry sheet in the dish, pat it against the sides and then slide it into the top part of the oven to cook for 6–8 minutes.
7 While the pastry is in the oven, wash the rhubarb and then cut it up into wedges no longer than half an inch/1 cm.
8 Toss the rhubarb pieces with the ginger jam and sultanas in an ovenproof dish.
9 When the pastry shell is just firm and pale brown,

remove it from the oven. Turn the oven down to Reg. 4 (350°F, 175°C).

10 Slip the rhubarb mixture into the oven and cook it (covered) for 45 minutes. By this time the rhubarb should just be tender (try it if you aren't sure).

11 Strain the rhubarb juices into a saucepan, sprinkle over the gelatine and dissolve over heat.

12 Heap the rhubarb into the pastry shell, pour over the juices and chill the tart for 3–4 hours to set the fillings.

Cakes and biscuits

Cakes and biscuits

It is time tea parties for grown-ups were revived. They can be friendly and relaxed occasions for seeing friends, and they require little planning and preparation. They have one other important asset: the delicious 'forbidden' foods of life can be enjoyed to the full, and incidentally it is worth being generous with them. First, margarine tastes differently from butter and is no substitute for it, so use butter to produce melt-in-the-mouth cakes and biscuits. Secondly, biscuits are made crisp by their sugar, and so it is wise to follow the quantities in the recipes. Lastly, go cautiously with flour because it has a tendency to make mixtures bland and heavy; indeed, it produces the opposite effect from butter, sugar and another binding agent, eggs.

It is a good idea to have all the ingredients and utensils ready before you begin, so you can complete the preparations without a break. This is important because neither cake nor biscuit mixtures can be left to stand around before their cooking. Thus it is best to remove butter from the fridge several hours in advance, to let it warm up to room temperature and become soft and malleable. Baking tins should be greased with butter, and cake tins too, and then coated with sugar to give the cooked cake a crisp outside. Lastly the oven should always be pre-heated so that the inside temperature is even everywhere. A constant temperature is needed for the cooking, and gusts of cold air can have fatal effects, particularly on a rising cake so beware of opening the oven door during the early stages of cooking while cakes, biscuits and meringues go through a liquid, fragile stage before they achieve their final, stable structure. Of course it's always necessary to take a look towards the end of the cooking time to see whether the goods are cooked and, in the case of cakes, to test them. This is done by inserting a sharp knife into the centre of the cake. If the cake is cooked, the knife will come out clean but if some mixture adheres to the blade, it is not quite ready.

CARDAMOM CAKE

It is a pity the excellent flavour of cardamom is so little known and appreciated.

This recipe yields a cake that will satisfy six hearty appetites.

Preparation time: 10–15 minutes
Cooking time: 1½ hours

¼ pt/140 ml milk
10 green cardamom pods
6 oz/170 g unsalted butter
9 oz/255 g caster sugar
3 eggs
8 oz/225 g self-raising flour
1 oz/30 g semolina
1 oz/30 g ground almonds
nob of butter for greasing cake tin and 1 tbs caster
   sugar

1 Turn the oven to Reg. 3 (325°F, 160°C).
2 Crush the cardamom pods (there is no need to remove the husks) and put them with the milk in a small pan. Bring the infusion to the boil, remove from the heat and allow it to sit for 15 minutes.
3 Grease a cake tin (medium size) with the butter and coat the surface with the sugar.
4 Meanwhile put the other butter and sugar in a mixing bowl and work them together so that they form a smooth, homogeneous cream – like brandy butter mixture.
5 Now incorporate one of the eggs, then sift in a third of the flour and repeat this process with the remainder of the flour and eggs.
6 Stir in the semolina and ground almonds.
7 Pour the cardamom-flavoured milk through a sieve into the cake mixture and stir it in too.
8 Fill the tin with the cake mixture and slip it into the middle of the oven to bake for 1 hour 20 minutes.
9 Test to see that the cake is cooked; if it is, remove it from the oven and let it sit for 15 minutes before turning it out onto a wire rack to dry and cool for about 2 hours.

LEMON CAKE

This recipe was given to me by my sister-in-law. It will make a delicious tea for about five people.

Preparation time: 10–15 minutes
Cooking time: 20–25 minutes

3 oz/85 g unsalted butter
3 oz/85 g caster sugar
1 egg
3 oz/85 g self-raising flour
1 lemon
2 heaped tbs caster sugar
a nob of butter and 1 dsp caster sugar for coating the
   baking tin

1 Set the oven to Reg. 5 (375°F, 190°C).
2 Prepare a small, shallow baking tin by greasing the bottom and sides with the butter and then shaking the sugar over it.
3 Grate the rind from the lemon. Then squeeze the juice from the two halves.
4 Pour the sugar into a mixing bowl and add the butter cut into pieces. Work the butter and sugar together so they form a smooth homogeneous cream.
5 Add the egg and mix it in. Now tip the flour through a sieve into the cake mixture. Add the lemon rind (you will use the juice later) and mix together very well for a minute or two.
6 Turn the mixture into the baking tin and smooth it down with a knife and place it in the upper part of the oven. Let the cake cook for twenty minutes.
7 While the cake is cooking, prepare the lemon infusion by mixing the juice with the 2 tbs caster sugar in a teacup.
8 Test to see if the cake is cooked – the top should be golden brown and the mixture set. If it isn't ready, give it another 5 minutes cooking.
9 Remove the cake from the oven and prick about half a dozen holes in the top.
10 Dribble the lemon juice mixture over the cake and then leave it to cool for about 20 minutes.
11 The cake should now be firm enough to remove from the tin. Go round the sides of the tin with a flat knife, making sure they will come away easily, and the bottom; then invert the cake onto a wire rack. Now repeat the operation but tip the cake onto your outstretched palm and then, right-side up, slide it back onto the tray. (The object of this rather lengthy exercise is to let the cake dry the right way up so that the lemon juice stays in the cake and the top of it is not marked with the wire-network of the drying rack.)

Let the cake cool down for about an hour before eating it.

GINGER LOAF

This is a hybrid cake, a cross between gingerbread and parkin, so it is rich with golden syrup and brown sugar, bolstered up with some oatmeal. It is no trouble to make and better if it is left to mature for a day before being eaten; it will feed six people easily.

Preparation time: 10–15 minutes
Cooking time: 1¼–1½ hours

4 oz/115 g unsalted butter
2 oz/55 g dark brown sugar
4 tbs (i.e. 8 oz/225 g) golden syrup
1 tbs ginger preserve/marmalade
3 eggs
6 oz/170 g self-raising flour
2 oz/55 g medium oatmeal
1 heaped tsp powdered ginger
1 level tsp allspice
nob of butter for greasing the cake tin

1 Turn the oven to Reg. 3 (325°F, 160°C).
2 Put the butter, brown sugar, golden syrup and ginger preserve into a large saucepan and melt them together gently.
3 Remove the pan from the heat and let the contents cool down for five minutes. Meanwhile grease the cake tin (medium size).
4 Add the flour, oatmeal and spices and then beat in the eggs, one by one. Mix everything together very well.
5 Pour the mixture into the baking tin and set it in the middle of the warm oven for an hour.
6 Look at the cake and test to see whether it is cooked; if it isn't ready, let it cook for another 10–15 minutes.
7 Remove the cake from the oven and leave it to cool for 15 minutes before turning it out onto a wire rack to dry off and cool to room temperature (this will take a couple of hours).

RICH FRUIT CAKE

When you make this for your family and friends, I hope you will convince them you are a very accomplished cook. If you omit the almonds, it can be covered with marzipan and icing to make a fine Christmas cake.

These quantities will give eight generous helpings but it keeps very well if you store it in an airtight tin. It is best made several days before it is needed.

Preparation time: 15–20 minutes
Cooking time: about 2½–3 hours

6 oz/170 g unsalted butter
3 oz/85 g caster sugar
3 oz/85 g brown sugar
3 eggs
6 oz/170 g self-raising flour
1 lemon
8 oz/225 g currants
8 oz/225 g sultanas
4 oz/115 g glacé cherries
4 oz/115 g diced mixed peel
1 level tsp mixed spice
2 tbs brandy
1 oz/30 g split or whole blanched almonds
a nob of butter and 1 tbs caster sugar for greasing the tin

1 Set the oven to Reg. 2 (315°F, 155°C).
2 Prepare the cake tin by rubbing the sides and bottom with the butter, then coating it with the sugar.
3 Grate the rind from the lemon and squeeze out its juice. Set on one side.
4 Begin the cake mixture by putting the butter and brown and white sugars in a mixing bowl and cutting up the butter with a knife. Then work the butter and sugars together so that they form a homogeneous cream.
5 Break an egg into the mixture and mix it in well. Then add, through a sieve, a third of the flour.

FLAPJACK

6 Repeat (5) with the other 2 eggs and the rest of the flour.

7 Now add the fruit: currants, sultanas, cherries, mixed peel, lemon rind, juice and also the mixed spice and brandy. Mix everything together very well with a wooden spoon.

8 Pour the mixture into the cake tin and smooth down the top.

9 Scatter the almonds over the cake and transfer it to the middle of the oven. Leave to cook for 2½ hours.

10 Test to see if the cake is ready; if it isn't, give it another ¼–½ hour.

11 Remove the cake from the oven. Allow it to stand for ½ hour in its tin so that it can cool down and become firm before you try to handle it.

12 Lift the cake from the tin and set it to cool on a wire rack. It will reach room temperature in 2–3 hours and be ready to eat.

Here's an old family recipe for these simple oat biscuits. They keep well for at least a week in an airtight tin.

This recipe yields about 15 flapjacks.

Preparation time: 10–15 minutes
Cooking time: 30 minutes

4 oz/115 g butter
4 oz/115 g soft brown sugar
4 oz/115 g porridge oats
1 oz/30 g self-raising flour

1 Set the oven to Reg. 4 (350°F, 175°C).
2 Use a nob of the butter (or an old butter paper) to grease the bottom and sides of a sandwich tin (approximately 7 inches/18 cm in diameter).
3 Melt the butter and sugar in a saucepan.
4 Stir in the oats and flour.
5 Turn the mixture into the tin and smooth out the top.
6 Put the tin in the oven and leave the flapjack to cook for half an hour.
7 At the end of the cooking time remove the biscuit from the oven and let it cool for about 10 minutes before you cut it into slices the size of new carrots. It will be quite cool in another ½–¾ hour, when you can remove the pieces with a spatula knife and eat them.

CHOCOLATE POLKA-DOT COOKIES

These are very good by themselves or with ice-cream. The recipe is sufficient for about 50 biscuits; they can be stored in an airtight container.

Preparation time: 10–15 minutes
Cooking time: 20–30 minutes

3 oz/85 g unsalted butter
3 oz/85 g granulated or caster sugar
3 oz/85 g soft brown sugar
1 egg
4 oz/115 g self-raising flour
few drops of vanilla essence
4 oz/115 g (1 packet) plain chocolate polka-dots
1 oz/30 g butter for greasing baking trays

1 Set the oven to Reg. 5 (375°F, 190°C).
2 First grease two baking trays with some butter. (The reserve will be used when you come to bake another round of biscuits.)
3 Put the butter and sugars in a bowl and cut up the butter into small pieces. Then work the butter and sugar together with a fork or electric beater to form a smooth cream.
4 Mix in the egg.
5 Add the self-raising flour, through a sieve, and vanilla essence and mix well once more.
6 Stir in the polka-dots.
7 With a teaspoon drop the mixture onto the trays allowing 2 inches/5 cm between each mound.
8 Transfer the tins to the top of the oven and leave the biscuits to cook for 7–8 minutes. They are ready when they have puffed up and then 'died' down and are a rich golden brown. (If the biscuits appear to have cooked unevenly on the tray in

future turn the trays around after the first 5 minutes and then proceed for a further 2–3 minutes cooking.)
9 Remove the tins from the oven and let the biscuits sit for half a minute. Then use a spatula knife to peel them delicately off the tin and place them on a wire rack to dry.
10 Wipe the tins clean and then repeat steps 1 and 7–9 with the remainder of the mixture.

VARIATIONS
These biscuits are also good made with a mixture of 2 oz/55 g chocolate polka-dots and 1½ oz/40 g almond flakes. For serving with fruit puddings, such as ice-cream, fruit salad or mousse, I think it is best to omit the chocolate altogether and just use 3 oz/85 g almond flakes.

SHORTBREAD

Preparation time: 10–15 minutes
Cooking time: 40–45 minutes

This recipe yields about 12 pieces.

4 oz/115 g unsalted butter
2 oz/55 g caster sugar
3 oz/85 g plain flour
1 oz/30 g rice flour
optional: **1 dsp caster sugar**

1   Set the oven to Reg. 3 (325°F, 160°C). Lightly grease a sandwich tin (approximately 7 inches/18 cm in diameter).
2   In a bowl, cream the butter and sugar together with a fork or electric beater.
3   Incorporate both kinds of flours and then spread the mixture in the tin; prick the surface in a few places and transfer to the middle of the oven for 40–45 minutes. The shortbread is ready when it is a very pale golden brown.
4   Remove from the oven and leave to cool for 5 minutes. Cut into pieces, and when it is cool sprinkle with sugar if you wish.

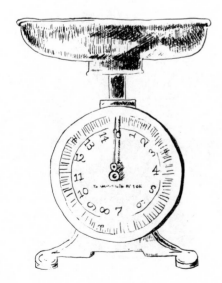

ALMOND MERINGUES

Meringues make a wonderful accompaniment to fruit salads and ice-creams, and they are also very good when they are glued together in pairs with whipped cream. I'm not sure why people think they are hard to make because it simply isn't true; indeed, they are one of the quickest and most rewarding sweet concoctions I can think of.

You will need some Bakewell paper (available from Boots) to line the baking trays.

This recipe yields about 30 meringues.

Preparation time: 10–15 minutes
Cooking time: 1½–2 hours

4 egg whites (separate the whites from the yolks by juggling them between the shells while pouring off the whites)
8 oz/225 g caster sugar
4 drops vinegar
2 oz/55 g almond flakes

1   Set the oven to Reg. ½ (280°F, 135°C).
2   Prepare the baking tins by lining two baking trays with pieces of Bakewell paper.
3   Put the egg whites in a bowl and whisk them up until they form stiff peaks. Don't go on beating the mixture after it has reached this stage because you can overbeat egg whites and make them collapse.
4   Add the vinegar (it helps to keep the meringue mixture together) and beat in the sugar very rapidly.
5   Stir in the almond flakes.
6   With a dessertspoon, place the mixture in spoonfuls on the trays. You can pack them together quite closely because they won't expand while they cook.
7   Put the trays in the middle of the oven and leave to cook for an hour. Reverse the trays if one set of meringues is looking a little brown and continue the cooking for a further half hour. See whether you can pull the meringues away from the paper without any trouble; if you can't, they need another ½ hour's cooking.
8   Transfer them to a wire rack and leave to cool.

Names and terms

ANCHOVY PURÉE: It is sold in tubes by many delicatessens and supermarkets.

BEAN CURD: Tofu is the Japanese name for this highly proteinaceous preparation of soya beans which has a texture reminiscent of baked egg custard. It is sold fresh in many health food shops and oriental stores, and can often be found tinned. It is used as a primary source of protein in vegetarian dishes, or to enrich some sauces and meat dishes.

BEAN SPROUTS: Fresh bean sprouts are widely available, and the canned ones are no substitute. Green mung beans are normally used for bean sprouts, and they are easy to grow. Sprinkle some beans onto a damp flannel or absorbent cloth, lay on a plate with a little water and leave in a warmish place to germinate and sprout. They should be ready in about a fortnight.

CARDAMOM: The dried green or white pods contain aromatic seeds which can be used in savoury dishes, puddings and cakes. The plant is a member of the ginger family.

CHEESES: Fresh, not pre-packed, English, French, Italian, Swiss and Scandinavian cheeses are now sold almost throughout the United Kingdom. Often English cheeses are the best buy for flavour and price. Cheddar and Stilton are the most famous of the English cheeses but there are many others: Red Leicester, Double Gloucester, Cheshire, Lancashire, Wensleydale, to name but a few. Recently some new cheeses have appeared such as Lymeswold, Cotswold and Rutland.

The French have many hundreds of cheeses to their name. Probably only 50 different kinds come to England, of which Brie is the most famous. Sadly, good Brie has become more and more difficult to obtain because there has been a tendency to produce a cheese that keeps for a long time, with the result that it never ripens properly. These Bries stand about one inch/2 cm high, while the proper Bries are much thinner, and usually yellower inside. There are many other wonderful French cheeses nonetheless: Roquefort (from sheep's milk), Camembert (but beware of non-ripening varieties too), Reblochon, Bleu de Bresse, Tomme, Vacherin, Pont l'Evêque and many more. A number of goats' cheeses are made in France, some of which are very pungent. For cooking, a milder cheese, like a slice from a Bûche log, is more suitable. There are also tiny cheeses marinated in oil and herbs called Pitchou.

Parmesan cheese can be bought either ready grated or in a block. The latter is considerably more expensive but its taste is far superior, and it keeps its flavour longer. Gorgonzola is a powerful Italian cheese, while Bel Paese is soft, creamy and gentle. Ricotta, made from sheep's milk, enjoys popularity now and Mozzarella is another mild cooking cheese, often found on the tops of pizzas.

Gruyère does not have holes in it (or only very small ones), but Emmenthal does. Both these Swiss cheeses have a fairly strong flavour which is excellent for cooking.

CHILLIS: Fresh green and red chillis are now widely available. They come in many different shapes and sizes: some are 'tiny devils', small green chillis that are very powerful, while others are bigger and milder. The quantities in the recipes are thus guidelines, and if you don't care for very spicy food, you might try using a little less on the first occasion.

COCONUT MILK: This is not the liquid inside a coconut. Coconut milk can be made either by boiling the white flesh of a fresh coconut in water and then straining off the liquid or more easily from powdered or creamed coconut. Both the latter are sold in many shops.

CORIANDER: The dried seeds are easily obtained, and the fresh leaf (parsley-like) is now finding its way into more and more shops. It has a delicate but fiery flavour; and its aroma is wonderful.

CUMIN: The seeds of *Cuminum cyminum* are either dull yellow or light brown, with a slightly acrid spicy flavour. They can be purchased dried, either whole or ground. It is an essential ingredient of curry powders, and many Eastern dishes.

DILL WEED: The feathery leaves of the garden herb, *Anethum graveolens*, can be bought dried or fresh. They have a more delicate flavour than the seeds, which are also easy to purchase.

GARAM MASALA: A wonderful collection of Eastern spices. There are many versions but the mixture is almost certain to include coriander seeds, cumin seeds, black pepper, cardamom seeds, cinnamon, cloves and nutmeg.

GARLIC: Fresh garlic really is far superior to dried garlic granules, and it is available almost everywhere. A head of garlic is composed of cloves.

GINGER: Fresh ginger root (brown and knobbly) is sold by most greengrocers and supermarkets and imparts a different flavour from the dried ground spice.

OILS: There are several kinds of cooking oils widely available: olive (extra virgin is the best), vegetable (blends of oils often containing soya and rapeseed), corn (maize), sunflower, sesame and peanut. Olive oil is essential for making a good salad dressing and it imparts a characteristic lushness to any dish which cannot be matched by vegetable or corn oil, though the latter are suitable for deep frying. Sunflower and peanut oil are both less rich and the latter is used a great deal in Eastern cooking. The unique flavour of sesame oil is best appreciated if it is added at the end of cooking, and not used for frying.

PEPPERCORNS: Black, white and green ones are sold dried in many shops. In these recipes I have favoured using green peppercorns in brine because they are softer, and pleasanter to eat, if they have only been roughly chopped rather than ground up.

PESTO: This Italian sauce of fresh basil leaves, olive oil, garlic, pine kernels (or walnuts), parmesan and seasoning has sprung to international fame in the last few years. It is easy to make at home in a food processor or liquidizer in the summer when fresh basil is available in the shops, and in the winter the ready-made varieties pass as adequate substitutes. Eat it with pasta.

ROUX: Butter and flour paste that forms the basis for white, and other similar, sauces.

STOCKS: Home-made stocks are really very little trouble to prepare. Chicken, beef, veal and ham bones make the best meat stocks (lamb and pork are too fatty), while salmon and cod heads, prawn, lobster or crab shells make excellent fish stocks. Simply pile some bones into a large pot (you can accumulate bones in the deep freeze) cover with water and set to boil for a couple of hours. Then strain the liquid through a sieve, cover with more water and add some salt. The first boiling will have removed some of the goodness and flavour from the bones, and the second salty mixture will remove more. When the stock is cold remove the fat coating if you wish, cover and store in the fridge, or freezer.

Index

Notes